FIVE STARS
IN THE
WINDOW

Growing Up during World War Two

BY DAVID KOMARNICKI

with illustrations by Amy Komarnicki

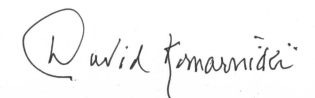

ISBN-13:
978-1544172385

ISBN-10:
1544172389

ACKNOWLEDGMENTS

God: for being the Lord of life's purpose and fulfillment.

Country: for welcoming two immigrants to plow, to plant, then harvest their dreams.

My parents, Joe and Anna: for giving me life and modeling life's standards.

My brothers and sisters: for sharing the tastes, the touches, and the warmth of my life.

Friends and strangers: for being nouns in search of the verbs of our times.

The City of Chester: for being the incubator of my meanderings and adventures.

My children: for being the authenticators of my treasure chest of hopes and ambition.

My wife, Leslie: for her loving partnership, inspiration, and encouragement and for using her consummate editorial skills to take the scribbles of my childhood reminiscences and help me fashion them into these printed words.

David Komarnicki
In the year of our Lord
December 2016

Contents

The Jawbreaker

Many decades after the stories in this book took place, my niece Robyn presented me with the momentous gift of a giant jawbreaker. She had long been a fan of my childhood reminiscences, and she knew the pivotal role that such sugar-laden confections from Charlie Peck's Emporium had played in my younger days—a role that had made several of my molars and incisors fall victim to the pliers of Dr. Mielcarek, our family dentist.

Mindful of the damage wrought in bygone days, I let the speckled orb sit untasted for months—until one afternoon, not long ago, nostalgia got the best of me.

*   *   *

Popping the jawbreaker into my mouth, moving it into the cushion of my cavernous jaw, I close my eyes and give forth a deep sigh of contentment. Sucking leisurely on the first layer, I am suddenly transported to the sanctum of a simpler time—a pre-Pearl Harbor Saturday on the streets of Chester, Pennsylvania. I see my own 13-

1

year-old image, emerging with candy-bulged pockets from the aforementioned Peck's Emporium, and I hear a familiar wail.

It's my youngest brother, cherub-faced Jimmy, tugging at his sagging knickers and calling to me plaintively, "Take me with you, Davey. I wanna go. I won't get in your way, I promise."

The shadowy image of my childhood self dashes up an alley and ducks behind a tree, watching my despondent brother turn back and trudge homeward, where Mom will be waiting with a peanut butter sandwich.

Jolted back to the present, I feel the "Jimmy layer" of my jawbreaker start to melt away.

"Come back, Jimmy! Come back. I'll give you my tailor-made suit with two pairs of pants. We'll ride the Bridgeport ferry across the Delaware. I'll carry you across the Chester Creek trestle. I'll give you a bag of jellybeans. Just holler after me again. I'll take you with me this time..."

"Nevermore," says my soul, and the Jimmy layer vanishes.

My saliva continues to work its magic on the still-giant jawbreaker, and suddenly I'm tasting the next layer. What's that I hear? Could it be the groans of Sylvester Wilson? It is. The image is unmistakable. Sylvester, a local kid, is locked in a marble shoot-out with my next-youngest brother, Paul, the left-handed Maestro of Marbledom.

I watch in awe as Paul knuckles down in a game of "hits and spans" and methodically empties his opponent's pockets. I see Sylvester slouching home and Paul scanning the playground for his next victim, and then the image begins to fade.

"Paul I'd give you my pearl-handled penknife if we could play marbles right now. I'd carry you piggyback to Lieperville Quarry if you'd just show me how to radar in on a marble six feet away."

"Time's up," memory whispers, as the Paul layer ebbs away.

My tongue pokes away at the jawbreaker, and suddenly I'm standing on the corner near Larkin Elementary, fingering my Dick Tracy cap gun and acting as an audience of one as brother George (next up from me in the 10-kid line-up) leapfrogs parking meters down Eighth Street. He turns and sees me watching, then beckons me to join him.

Mimicking George's Tom Mix swagger, I cross the street and follow him into the heady aroma of Roy Reiser's Cigar and Tobacco Store. Tired, bald-headed Roy drags himself to the counter, and George asks with exaggerated politeness, "Do you have Prince Albert in a can?"

Roy squints at us. "Yes, I do, son," he growls, "but you're too young to buy it."

Suppressing our chortles, we head for the screen door. "We don't want to buy it, Mr. Reiser. We just want you to let Albert out of the can!"

George slams the screen door, and I unload six caps in Roy's direction. We take off running towards Edgmont Avenue, when suddenly I feel the George layer of my jawbreaker fading away.

"Slam the door once more, George, and laugh your way with me down the Eighth Street of my mind. Let's goad the priest at St. Michael's Rectory into a chase he can't win. Let's make Kandravi the traffic cop blow his whistle for riding two on a bike through town. I'll even spend my last nickel to buy you a lead soldier at

McCrory's if you'll let me wear your Philadelphia A's baseball hat. Wait up, George! Wait up!"

The image disappears behind a tree: "Can't wait," it calls to me.

I shift my jawbreaker to my left cheek. And there I am—standing in front of the display window at Briggs Sporting Goods, my reflection superimposed upon a Wilson baseball cushioned in a Ted Williams fielder's mitt.

Suddenly I see my 17-year-old brother, Dan, staring back at me from inside the store. The door opens, and he darts out, bouncing a genuine Nat Holman basketball.

We walk toward the YMCA together, and Danny lets me take the ball as we pass Speare Brothers Department Store. The quartz flecks in the sidewalk flash like jewels in the sun as I dribble across Seventh Street to the Y steps. Dan retrieves his ball, and we descend into the basement locker room, where the suffocating odor of 200 unwashed sweat socks greets us.

Danny changes into his Glen Burnie Aces uniform, and we make our way into the gym. While he goes through his warm-up routine, I vault myself to the top of the parallel bars—the perfect vantage point for catching the athletic prowess of my big brother at work in the upcoming semi-final game against rival Parkside.

Then Eddie Morrell sounds the buzzer, and the game begins. Danny has the ball. He fakes to the left. He stoops. He shoots. The slow-motion arch curves downward, swishing through the net 20 feet away. The crowd roars. As I watch from my perch, sights, sounds, odors, touch, and taste mingle with a sense of atomic implosion: adroit hands bouncing the basketball; muscle-rippled calves flexing to microsecond messages from the brain; the piercing shrill of a referee's whistle; raucous reactions from the crowd as they praise or protest his call.

4

I see Danny stealing the ball, streaking for a lay-up in mid-air, right arm extended, the ball released. Then suddenly the whole scene turns to shadow. The Danny layer of my jawbreaker is dissolving.

"Come back, Danny. I'll serve your mail route through Garden City for two days if I can relive this game and find out the final score. I'll stuff your Sunday papers chest-high at the Great Leopard skating rink if I can watch the smile rise on your face again after that deceptive steal."

"Game's over," says time's referee.

I feel another jawbreaker layer emerging in my now multi-colored mouth. Who's that I see? It's big brother Joe walking by. How can a guy always look so neat, so poised and in control? And that gorgeous blonde on his arm should be in an Andy Hardy movie. I heard Joe call her Doris. They look happy together, not mushy-happy, just excited-happy, happy to be alive.

Joe's Doris walks the way that Doris Day sings— with a bounce, a smile, and a whispered sigh, all in tune. Her saddle shoes are neatly polished, her bright hair is parted in the middle, her eyes fixed in anticipation of the next moment—as if a breakaway touchdown is about to take place, and she's the captain of the cheerleaders. Joe quietly acknowledges that all within sight are his friends—you can see it by his easy smile and stride. No wonder he was president of his class last year.

I watch them as they hand-hold their way down the street. Are they heading to Boyd Drugs for a cherry coke or maybe to the Deshong Art Gallery for a walk through the paintings? As they reach the intersection of Seventh and Edgmont, I wonder if life will ever merge for me that way, the way they are right now, two hearts with a single beat? A lump rises in my throat, as memory resurrects a song I'd heard on the jukebox at Charlie Peck's: "The girl

5

that I marry will have to be as sweet and as soft as a nursery ..." ("And wear saddles shoes and pleated skirts," I add to the lyrics.)

The lump in my throat recedes, and I become aware again of the jawbreaker in my mouth. It seems smaller. I inspect it surreptitiously and see that the Joe layer is vanishing.

"Come back, Joe. Take the helm of the Chester High student body again and squire your sweetheart down the streets of town on a Saturday afternoon. I'll polish your shoes and hers, too, if you'll just stroll by again hand in hand."

"So long, little brother," says Joe as he and Doris duck around the corner.

My multicolored tongue prods the jawbreaker once more, and I'm transported to the front of Weinberg's Department Store. The class-conscious of Chester and environs look to Sol Weinberg's store as the mecca of fashion, and my Levi's and T-shirt look out of place in the throng of window-browsers.

Suddenly I spot the slender ankle of a familiar leg as sister Vicky strolls through the hallowed doors for a tour of wishful thinking. I follow at a safe distance. Maybe I'll discover a special thing she longs for, garner my Christmas Club money, and lavish her with a present she'll never forget.

With the heart of Sir Galahad, I slink along behind and watch my beloved sister pull a white-collared dress from the rack. She holds it in front of her and gazes at her reflection in a three-way mirror: her hair neatly parted at the side; a ribbon tucked around a strand; her doe-brown eyes smiling as she inspects her image from the left, the right, and the center.

After a lingering stop at the fine-jewelry counter,

Vicky moves on to the cosmetics department. Daintily squeezing the atomizer of a sample bottle of perfume, she lightly sprays her left wrist and raises it to the judgment of nostrils able to enjoy aromas the purse cannot afford. The powder puffs, the bubble baths, the carved soaps— nothing escapes her wistful eye, her cautious touch, her secret yearning.

Vicky leaves Weinberg's the way she came, filled with mental pictures of what might be hers in some magical tomorrow. A pensive happiness lights her unlined face; her eyes dance; her step is light as she walks empty-handed out of the store.

I feel the Vicky layer of my jawbreaker melting away.

"Come back, Vicky. I want to see you finger the fabric in the Weinberg racks again and linger over the gold bracelets on the jewelry counter. I'll buy you a year's supply of scented soap and even let you have first dibs on the bathtub."

The trim ankles disappear around the corner.

I suck hard on the jawbreaker that's steadily dwindling away in my mouth. Another layer of sweetness sends signals to my taste buds, and I'm whisked away to the sidewalk in front of McCrory's Five & Dime.

In the distance, half-hidden by a road-hogging trolley car, I see the unmistakable grill of a panther-sleek 1936 Ford. I drink it in as it approaches: gangster whitewalls, mirror-bright black paint reflecting whatever it passes. My heart beats to the rhythm of a Gene Kruppa drum each time I see a car like this. Could it be? No. Yes, it is! It's brother John behind the wheel!

The clang of the trolley grinding on its steel track, the steam thrusts of a train with endless box cars, the flagrant horn of a cab in pursuit of a destination labeled

"Hurry!"—all converge to drown out my raucous shout after John. Windows rolled up, steel-blue eyes riveted on the traffic ahead, he passes without noticing me.

How many are the times I'd watched him tap-dance his way down the three front steps of our house, doing his Bojangles soft-shoe shuffle? How often had I rehearsed the confident way he stands before a mirror or tried on his size 40 blazers, hoping someday he'd pass one or two of them on to me? But more than his dapper clothes, I yearn to inherit his style, his smile, his gift and zest for life, his Errol Flynn flair, his fearless stare.

The John layer of my jawbreaker is starting to crumble.

"Come back, Johnny. I'll put shoetrees in all your loafers and give you my entire set of 'Horrors of War' cards if I can hop into the front seat with you and ride around the streets of Chester for just one golden afternoon."

But the Ford disappears around the dogleg turn onto Market Street, giving one last staccato horn-honk before passing out of sight under the railroad station.

I suck again on the jawbreaker remnants, and suddenly I'm standing in front of the Great Leopard Skating Rink, checking out the crowd that's gathered to enter this magic world of music and motion. A pony-tailed girl in pleated skirt, pink sweater, and brown-and-white saddle shoes is leaning adoringly on her boyfriend's arm. His black woolen jacket is crested with a large letter "C" imprinted with a football—a witness to all that he's varsity. Then I see a familiar figure toward the front of the line—a reed-slim, well-muscled body on nimble legs.

"There's brother Mickey!" I yell. Just then the line surges forward, carrying my oldest brother through the entrance. I'm sure that he's taking the steps two by two so that he can whip through the business of renting his skates and get out on the floor to match his inner tune with the ever-changing melodies of the organist.

I want to exchange my last dime for a ticket and climb those same stairs, then stand unobserved in a corner to watch Mickey skate his Saturday into the record book, his hands linked with those of his girlfriend, Myra Grey. I know they'll be in perfect tune with the music as they circle the outer edge of the rink—forward, now backward, legs crossing legs, as happy together as a hand in a warm glove. But before I can pull my coin out of my pocket, I feel the Mickey layer of my jawbreaker dissolving into sweet liquid.

"Come back, Mickey! Flip hamburgers and pancakes again at the Boyd Diner. Sign my report card when my marks are too shameful to show Mom or Pop. Let me hear the roll of the Coke bottle on the bedroom floor as you work away your foot cramps from too much skating . . ."

But the organ at the Great Leopard stops playing, and my giant jawbreaker has turned into a mere nugget. I work my tongue to get one last taste of its sweetness.

In an instant, I am in the postage-stamp yard outside our home on East Seventh Street. I hear voices through the kitchen window, then the creaking of the hinges on the Coldspot refrigerator as somebody opens the door. No mistaking it, Mom and sister Mary are cooking up something special. The heat of the oven carries its secret to my quivering nostrils.

I peer cautiously through the window. Mary, the eldest of us all, stands apron-clad beside the open oven door, shifting the mound of *halupki* (cabbage-wrapped meat and rice), recycling the juice, testing the taste of this labor of love. My stomach rumbles as I watch Mary and Mom together in the kitchen, preparing in hours what we will devour in minutes.

Mary had recently married four-sport ace Jimmy Turk and settled into an apartment several blocks away. She was a walking reward, and chocolate cakes rolled endlessly from her mixing bowl. She had stood on the other side of Mom and supported my first shaky baby steps. Her thumb bore the pinpricks of more diaper changes than a nurse running an orphanage. She had washed me behind the ears, prayed over my mumps-swollen jaws, and wrapped me in scarves through many a storm-filled winter. She had forgiven me when I cracked the mirror in her rouge kit and accepted my yearly gift of Evening in Paris cologne with a moist eye and a hug of gratitude.

Mary turned suddenly toward the kitchen window. "David!" she said with her unique intonation, affection built into each syllable of my given name. The inner core of my jawbreaker is laid bare, and the last remnant disappears, taking the Mary layer with it.

"Come back, Mary! Buckle my galoshes again. Bake me a chocolate cake. I'll give you a gallon of perfume next year."

But the aroma of stuffed cabbage recedes, and the voices fade away . . .

And then in an eye-blink I am standing in front of my bureau again, my hair turned to silver, my legs still strong but no longer capable of running through the streets of Chester in a single Saturday afternoon.

The jawbreaker Robyn gave me is gone, and so are all the years between that innocent pre-Pearl Harbor day and now. But the memories remain, and they are sweet.

The Komarnicki family was brought together for a rare group photo before the oldest boys started heading off for war duty. In the back row (from left) are David, George, Joe, Mickey, John, Dan, and Paul. In the next row are Vicky, Mom (Anna), Pop (Joseph), and Mary. In the front is the youngest of the family, Jimmy. The photograph was taken by Kolasinski's, Chester, Pa., in 1942.

Gift of a Lifetime

Somebody asked me a ponderable question the other day about the who, what, how, and when of the beginning of my romance with the harmonica. And suddenly, as if in a dream sequence, the long-forgotten answers unfolded like sections of a well-peeled grapefruit, sour on my mental taste buds but invigorating to my soul. The answer is that my brother George was the one who gave me my first harmonica and started, with that one generous act of brotherly love, my sentimental journey with that sweet-sounding instrument.

The romance began on a Monday morning after the toughest, meanest, most life-threatening weekend of my unfolding life. Fleshing out the weekend's discordant details may bring on a fit of hyperventilation, but I'll chance it.

The story begins on Friday morning, about a week before school ended and summer began. Wanting to look my best, I borrowed George's brown, crepe-soled shoes, gave them a spit shine, and began lacing them up. Then—WHAMMO!—a shoestring broke, and it took me five minutes to even up the string and re-lace the eyelets. From here on out, it was uphill all the way. Bursting out of the house, I was halfway up Deshong Street when, frisking my pockets, I discovered my yo-yo was missing. I turned, ran home again, retrieved it from the White Owl cigar box I kept it in, and, like a Jesse Owens in full flight, made it to Larkin Grammar just as the bell tolled.

Today was to be my coronation day! At school assembly, I was featured to perform my full bag of yo-yo tricks that had nabbed the neighborhood championships. The entire school, grades one through six plus faculty, would be there. Attendance was mandatory, I was told. When everyone assembled in the auditorium, I noticed the janitor, Mr. Harkins, leaning on a broom in the rear. Just then Mrs. Good lifted her perfect-pitch whistle from its permanent position around her neck and blew a needle-sharp high-C above middle, which immediately squelched the noise level of the captive kids. Then, with modulated clarity, she rattled off an introductory résumé of my yo-yo exploits.

Blushing with pride, I vaulted from my onstage seat and, with a flair of professionalism, launched into my rigorous routine. The first- and second-graders, forced to sit up front, gasped with astonishment—especially when the "Shooting Star" became a "Three-Leaf Clover" leading to an "Around the World" maneuver. Encouraged by the oohs and aahs, I launched into my "Loop the Loop" routine, a perfect finale that got kids involved in the count. Then, just when the crowd had counted with me to 55 consecutive loops, the string broke.

I watched in horror as my diamond-studded yo-yo flew high above the heads of an admiring sea of faces— and came to rest right on top of the bristling, Little Orphan Annie head of my classmate Blossom Worrel. Miss Ginter, my homeroom teacher, and Miss Webb, librarian, rushed to Blossom's rescue as she lay sprawled in her seat, eighth row center. From triumph to tragedy in one faulty loop!

Assembly was dismissed for early recess, and Barney Massi, Tommy McAlooso, Fred Parker, and Mike Tatarelli, immediately cornered me, accusing me of fraying the string to make it break. I denied it, but they kept it up until the bell rang.

After school, feeling a little let down, I kicked a pebble all the way down Deshong Street. (I forgot that I was wearing George's good shoes.) Deciding to reward myself, I dropped by Charlie Peck's, laid my last nickel on his counter, and bought a bag of chocolate-covered bolsters.

Just as I stepped out of the store, already crunching happily away on my purchase, one of the molars in my lower right jaw cracked wide open. No doubt about it, a big piece of tooth was visible in the bolster bar when I yanked it out of my mouth for closer inspection. Running home, I cornered Mom and opened wide for her to assess the damage. Without hesitation, she scooped two crumpled dollar bills from her apron pocket and walked me to the front door with urgency, instructing me to run to Dr. Leopold Mielcarek's dental office at 531 Broad Street.

Not exactly eager to sit in the dreaded dental chair, I started off with more of a saunter than a run, but by the time I got to the Methodist Church at Seventh and Madison the growing pain caused me to adjust my pace to a double strut. By the time I made it to Saint Paul's Episcopal at Ninth and Broad, I was invoking Heaven to numb the throb. At Upland Street I noticed a sleek, black hearse pulling into Clancy's Funeral Parlor.

"More tears are shed on this corner for departing friends and family than I'll experience in a lifetime," I reflected, as I waited for a trolley to turn onto Upland.

15

The clock in D'Ignazio's window, as reliable as their tailored stitch, informed me as I passed that I had five minutes before Dr. Mielcarek's classic extracts came to a halt for the day. I sped on to Potter, checked traffic both ways, passed Third Presbyterian Church, then Moyamensing Fire Station, and without breaking stride ran until I turned the bronze knob on the heavy, beveled-glass door of the "tooth eliminator."

Dr. Mielcarek wasted no time on pleasantries but instead guided me right into his chair, fastened a napkin around my neck, and expertly spread my jaws with thumb and index finger for a quick survey. Without comment or background music, he selected his stainless-steel, heavy-duty pliers, eyeballed the cratered remains of my molar, braced both feet like an anchor man in a tug of war contest, then yanked.

With that single move, the good doctor introduced me to a level of pain I'd heretofore seen only on the face of a celluloid cowboy while he bit down on a towel and had a bullet dug out of his shoulder with a penknife.

"Bite down on this, kid. It will stifle the bleeding."

These were Dr. Mielcarek's exact words as he packed the vacancy with cotton. No pat on the head. He matter-of-factly wrapped the extracted tooth in the bloody napkin that had shackled my neck during the ordeal and held it out to me. I handed him the two crumpled bills and slumped my way out the door, moaning.

My first upward glance caught the Mac Theatre marquee across the street: *Charlie Chaplin: The Gold Rush*. I had seen the movie last Saturday and had laughed so hard I'd fallen backwards over the seat. But that was last week, I mumbled to myself, and even remembered laughter wasn't enough to displace my present Mielcarek-induced pain. Checking sidewalk cracks as I walked, I headed east on Ninth Street. When

I reached Upland Street, Carl Kateski popped out of RHEA's Drug Store, hailed me down, and monologued me into Clancy's Funeral Parlor. At the far end of the viewing room was an open casket, surrounded by a wall of flowers, and the sight of the deceased immediately paralyzed everything but my imagination. This viewing of the departed was my first ever.

Carl whispered something unintelligible as I focused on the casket through fear-infused tears. The body seemed to slowly rise to an angled 45-degree posture. I swallowed hard, backing towards the double entry doors, but I failed to see Carl slip out—clicking the exit doors shut, leaving me alone in the room. I grappled with the door, but Carl held it shut from the outside. Just then a pear-shaped man in a gray suit entered through a side door and gently escorted me out another way—a merciful reprieve from reality therapy. I scanned the vicinity around Larkin School, but Carl was out of sight. He had definitely shown me something that temporarily took my pain away, but at the same time he'd introduced me to future nightmares.

This thought racked my aching head as I passed Jacob's Deli at the corner of Eighth and Deshong. Halfway down the dogleg of an alley, I spotted the black, multi-lacquered paddy wagon of the Chester Police. The police had raided an illegal crap game held in the huge warehouse, and the gamblers they'd caught were being packed like sardines into the wagon to be hauled four blocks to headquarters. I waited till the wagon pulled away, hoping to eyeball some local notables I knew from my nightly rounds huckstering *Philadelphia Records* and *Inquirers* around town.

I finally entered our house, feeling overwhelmed by all I'd been through that day. Mom was waiting in the kitchen with a gallon of sympathy and a bowl of Campbell's chicken noodle soup, accompanied by a

Fleischmann's yeast square and a tablespoon of castor oil (the latter two a universal cure for ailments).

I lay down on the living room couch, hot water bottle pressed to one cheek, the other feeling the prickly bristles of the horsehair couch, and listened with Mom to her favorite radio program, *The Johnson Family*. As the master of many voices made Mom ripple with hand-clapping laughter, I almost forgot that a major molar was gone forever from the lineup of crunchers dedicated to the breakdown of candied delights.

That evening, health somewhat restored, I made my newspaper-hustling rounds, squirreling in and out of my usual haunts:

- 520 Club

- Palm Gardens

- Penn Club

- State House Restaurant

- Boyd Diner

- Keenan's Bar

- Minnetti's Bar

- Chester Arms Hotel

- Pennsy Railroad Station

I had just vaulted down the steps of the Chester Club at Fifth and Welsh, two newspapers left to peddle, when a short, squatty man walking towards Fourth Street said, "What you got there, kid?"

"Philadelphia papers—a *Record* and an *Inquirer*."

"I'll buy both if you follow me. I got the money in my apartment."

I followed him around the corner, entered the dimly lit entrance to a hallway smelling of bacon grease, and

18

walked halfway up the stairs when suddenly a voice in my head shouted, "Run! Get out of here! Run!"

I turned, grabbed the banister with my right hand, and jumped six steps to the landing below, twisting my right ankle in the process, opened the entrance door, and fled, limping, for three blocks, to Sixth and Welsh. It struck me, while hobbling home, why a man might pretend he didn't have a dime in his pocket to buy my papers and had to take me to his room to get it. Pop had taught me to be wise like a serpent, and this wisdom had whispered to me and kept me out of harm's way.

Bathed and bedded down, I reflected on the day as I lay listening, as always, to the Eagle Café piano repertoire that bled through the bay windows. My ankle had swollen slowly like an inner tube being blown up one breath at a time. I stuffed my molar under my pillow (hoping for a visit from the Tooth Fairy). My sore gums sang an ode to a lost warrior sacrificed in the daily battle to crunch bolsters. As if timed to soothe the aching gap in my jaw, *"You are lost and gone forever, oh, my darling Clementine"* floated through the window.

Just then blood began to trickle in drops past my huge tonsils. I bit harder on the cotton plug. The trickle continued. An hour later it was still trickling, and, almost too feeble to cry out, I grabbed brother George's shoulder. His look of mingled shock and horror at the sight of the blood is etched in my memory forever. He got Mom. Mom called John. John called Chester Hospital on our newly installed Bell Telephone party line. The ambulance came faster than the Lone Ranger could shout "Geronimo." I was too weak from blood loss to walk, and John carried me down the steps and rode with me to the hospital. They had dripped three pints into my left arm by morning, and I regained consciousness in a white bed. A nurse with a starched white bonnet attended my every need, except food and water. I craved water like a

19

crippled camel in the Sahara Desert, and I pantomimed my drought to the nurse. She smiled an emphatic "No!" to my request as she readjusted the glucose bottle dripping vitals into my left arm, propped my pillows, and departed to attend to other outcries.

The next two hours were spent strategizing how to unplug from the I.V., climb out of bed, and sidle over to the Sun Rock watercooler across the room near the door. I timed arrivals and departures of the nurses, and when the wall clock had climbed toward 12 noon I detached, de-bedded, and maneuvered to a standing position. Weak but resolute, a loose dressing gown revealing my hinder parts, I used the three beds to my right as a banister to walk to the far wall. I made it undiscovered to the cooler, thumbed the faucet knob, and gorged on the arched water stream.

Waterlogged, proud that I had beaten the system, I staggered back to my bed. In route, wooziness joined vertigo, my eyes blurred, and then, just as my left knee touched the mattress, *it happened*. A volcanic upheaval of every detachable solid, every coloration of bile, every particle of hot dog, candy bar, Campbell's chicken noodle soup, and castor oil buried in any crevice of my stomach, gallbladder, or upper duodenum belched onto the bed sheet.

Only it was not *my* bed. The lava flow ricocheted off the belly of the man on the bed to my right. Florence Nightingale came running from her station in the hallway. With two assistants, she led me with gentle determination back to my bed. They washed me head to toe as if preparing me for viewing in Clancy's Funeral Parlor, re-needled my arm, and with gentle fervor reminded me of my breach of hospital etiquette. The old codger next to me was wheeled out of the room. The sheet was not pulled over his head, so I whispered a prayer for his recovery.

Brother John arrived just before dinner that evening to spring me from the hospital. At home I enjoyed all the spoils Mom could lavish on me and bedded down early, still too weak to focus.

Sunday morning brother Dan wrapped my sprained ankle, and I limped to church, mandatory even for the walking wounded. I listened attentively to the sermon and was especially moved by Walter Budnick's harmonica solo of "On the Old Rugged Cross" (Mom's favorite) and Danny Bartkow's epic, baritone rendition of "The Ninety-Nine Sheep." It seemed as though Danny looked right at me during all four verses.

Back at home, my tongue still checking out the massive empty space in my gum line, I trickled down a liquid lunch while sitting quietly in the kitchen, drawing giant four-leaf clovers on the oil cloth covering the kitchen table.

"Boy, do I need a shot of luck," I thought.

After dutifully carrying my empty soup bowl to the sink, I opened the back door to see if I could find a shamrock among the patchy grass in our 15' x 20' backyard. (Mom and I had searched one day, and she'd found two. We'd sealed them in a jelly jar for good luck). Well, I searched on bended knee till grass stains began to show, searched until I heard the unmistakable tooth-fanged growl of Rinnie, Sonny Lynch's German police dog, nemesis of the neighborhood.

I turned to catch sight of Rinnie just as he leaped the slatted wood fence between our yards. I ran to the far corner of the yard to hide behind the telephone pole, but Rinnie clenched my arm, ripping out a sizeable morsel of muscle and skin, and then re-arched a leap to his own side of the fence.

My scream, equal to Mrs. Good's perfect-pitch whistle, beckoned brother John. He reached for a

21

hanging shirt on the clothesline, ripped the sleeve into strips, and applied a tourniquet to my blood-gushing arm. When the bleeding stopped, John told me to sit still. He grabbed our garden hose, leaped the fence as smoothly as a high-hurdle champ, faced down Rinnie on the run, then, greeting the dog with jungle justice, lavished blows on it with a rubber hose.

John then re-leaped the fence, scooped me up, ran to the middle of the street, and hailed the first car heading towards town. As we pushed our way into the back seat of the car, John shouted, "Chester Hospital Emergency Ward!"

We sped through town, ignoring the piercing whistle of Officer Kandravi, the cop who maestroed the pulse beat of Chester's traffic. When we finally pulled up to the E.R. entrance on Upland Avenue, John kicked open the hospital's double doors, laid me on a gurney, and wheeled me into the emergency room. Florence Nightingale couldn't believe her eyes. We caught her as she sauntered down the hallway toward us.

In disbelief, she exclaimed, "Is it really you? Again?"

She took over the gurney, wheeling it into a workable area, and listened intently as John briefed her on the episode. I remember four faces huddled above me as Florence Nightingale stung me in the hindquarters with a shot. She then strapped a pint of blood on a pole, pumped up a prominent vein, and plugged a drip needle into my aching arm. I asked for a glass of water. She responded with a silent smile as she gazed at John in distracted admiration. I lay there looking up as four blue eyes built a bridge across my gurney.

Hmmm...could this be the reason why Rinnie bit me?

Apparently not. Instead of being wheeled off to the ward for overnight rehab and an opportunity for a Nurse Nightingale/Brother John romance to blossom, I was released after four hours in the emergency room.

That night, bedded down, hovering in the twilight zone, I cataloged my wretched condition: a throbbing sprain of the ankle, a yawning gap in the gum line, a shot in the buttock, a cratered hole in my right arm big enough to bury a bolster bar, three pints of new blood trying to integrate with my old blood, and a double dose of self-injected pity.

Just then, as I moved my arm instinctively upward under my goose-feathered pillow, I touched, then fisted, a miniature box. Holding it up for inspection, aided by the street lamp, I read the label: "Hohner Harmonica." Lifting the lid, I felt the smoothly polished silver housing of this tactile apparition of a longed-for dream. All pain vanished as I drifted into contented anticipation of Monday morning. Pop departed the room at 6:00. Brother George left at 7:30 for school, and I remained in bed for the day, searching for the tunes hidden somewhere between the sharps and flats, inner-ear sensitivity, and words and music buried deep within and aching for harmonic expression.

In time, I came to know that George slipped it under my pillow, though to this day he won't admit it. Perhaps as we sat side-by-side in the squeaky church pew, he saw the longing in my eyes when Walter Budnick, hands cupped around his Hohner, wailed away on his repertoire of hymns. Whatever motive prompted the gift, lost as it may be in George's rust-laden layers of amnesia, the gift was not lost. It has given rhythm and rhyme to the sentiments of my soul ever since.

For Everything a Time . . .
If Not a Reason

I have few memories of one-on-one conversation with Pop. He normally worked 10 hours a day (except, of course, for Sunday), and there was little time left for small talk with number eight in his line of 10 children. But we did talk occasionally, just the two of us, and one such meeting of our minds was really "big talk" over a very small issue.

It took place on a particular Friday evening outside the bedroom he shared with me and my brother George. It was my usual habit to slink into the room on cats' paws, creeping past Pop's white-enameled bed, which—thanks to the street lamp outside our bay window—cast a shadow like prison bars on the flower-papered wall. Once huddled into the small space left over from George's sprawl on our shared bed in the far corner of the room, I'd prop my pillow up so I could observe Pop. He'd lie flat on his back, inhaling air through his nostrils, then exhaling little breath-puff explosions—his rhythmic routine as regular as the movement of the hands on his faithful Bulova vest-pocket watch.

Many, many nights I'd lie in that corner, entertained by the nocturnal noises of Chester seeping through the lace curtains as I waited for sleep. I could hear the drone of the trolley as it advanced down Market Street one block west and the subtle click of cleated shoes touching down on the smooth sidewalk in front of the Eagles Club across the street. From inside the Eagles I could hear the piano player romancing the keys with a repertoire of Irish tunes, polkas, love songs, and ballads, all of them embedded in the psyches of sentimental patrons trying to drown out, with each elevation of the elbow, the pains of the current war.

But back to what I was saying about conversing with Pop on that fateful Friday evening. I was leaning on the stair rail outside our second-floor bedroom, just having finished lacing up the new high-tops I'd bought with money earned from peddling newspapers. There's a special surge of strength that kids get from inhaling the pungent aroma of new shoe leather, but this pair of high-tops packed a whammy that went beyond the norm. On the outside of the right shoe, about three inches below the top eyelet, was a penknife pouch, and in it was a shining-new, pearl-handled beauty. I pulled it out, fingers and thumb gliding across its smooth surface, and I felt a sensation beyond words as I reflected on all the uses possible with my Very Own Pocketknife.

Just then Pop stepped through the bedroom doorway, dressed for town and wearing a smile as bright as his dapper tie. But the smile faded quickly as he spotted the penknife in my hand. He eased tenderly into fatherly reasons why a pocketknife, in my possession, would not be a healthy thing, and I sensed by his deliberate tone and the logical progression of his

26

rationale where this would end. I waited respectfully for a pause, and when it came I countered, "But, Pop, the knife came with the high-tops."

I pointed to my right calf. "See, there's a pocket for it right here. Can't you see it? The shoes wouldn't look right if the knife weren't in there. And they wouldn't fit right either. The laces can't tighten with the right torque if the pocket's empty."

The word "torque" seemed to puzzle Pop, but he heard me out. Perhaps he was reflecting on his own boyhood on the family farm back in the Ukraine and wishing he'd had a pair of high-tops as he'd followed the cows back to the barn, his feet making a sucking sound each time he pulled them out of the thick mud that oozed above his shoe tops. I tried to appeal to the long-covered-up kid in him, and when that didn't work I presented the argument that times had changed since he'd been a boy milking the cows.

"Every kid has a penknife, Pop," I told him. "What can I tell them at school if I don't have one?"

I mustered every appeal I could stutter out and held it up before his Supreme Court of reason, but neither emotion nor logic worked. So I tried a detour into economics, reminding him that I'd bought the shoes myself with earnings from my nightly meanderings of child labor. I even appealed to authority, blurting out, "Mom said it was okay!" (This was not strictly true, however. Mom knew about the high-tops but not about the package deal that came with them).

Like a shipwrecked sailor losing his grip on his life preserver, I sank down the wall to sit on the patchy linoleum floor. Pop followed me down, dropping to one knee in order to maintain eye contact. My last ploy was a series of facial contortions, such as I'd witnessed in an Andy Hardy movie at the State Theatre where Mickey

Rooney was begging Lewis Stone for something equally vital to a kid's well-being. But Pop was a visionary, and he saw beyond my present grief to arguments unsolvable by pacifism, situations calling for urgent self-defense, and eventually to bloody street fights. I saw the same set of his jowls and the same look in his eyes that he'd worn the night he'd marched us into the cellar and had us toss George's Red Ryder BB gun into the flaming furnace.

Pop had a compartment in his mind labeled "Harm's Way," and once he put something there it was there to stay. The pearl-handled beauty would be joining items such as the BB gun and firecrackers and activities such as throwing rocks at each other, wielding ice picks in simulated war games, and family fistfights. The aforementioned activities usually met with welt-raising strappings in proportion to the offense, and Pop often quoted chapter and verse to show that his judgments came from a higher source: "He who spares the rod (or strap) hates his son (David), but he (Pop) who loves him is careful to discipline him."

In severe cases, he had a double-whammy from King Solomon: "If you punish with the rod, your son will not die. Punish him with the rod and save his soul from death." After much pondering, I'd concluded that it was good that Pop was taking my soul so seriously, but he sure was raising a lot of welts on my body to save it!

And so my triple-bladed, pearl-handled knife was confiscated that evening by the outstretched hand of Pop. I placed it in his palm with agony akin to when my tonsils had been snipped away on the operating table of Chester Hospital by Dr. Gallagher. Ah, but into my hand Pop placed a shiny half-dollar—compensation for the current misery and the sleepless nights that would follow.

Over the next few days I worked hard to assuage my anguish, judiciously eking out the half-dollar with treats from Charlie Peck's Ice Cream Emporium across the street. By Friday the reparations had run out, and though my stomach was full I still felt an emptiness in my heart for the confiscated treasure. That very afternoon, however, while I was walking down Deshong Street after school, Dudley Wilson challenged me to a marbles shoot-out in his side yard next to Massi's Parking Lot. I accepted and, with all the focus a malcontent kid can bring to a game, I cleaned him out. My pockets were stuffed to overflowing. Just before his mom hollered him inside for supper, Dudley reached down, unsnapped the side pocket on his high-tops, pulled out a pearl-handled penknife, and handed it off to me in exchange for the restoration of his marbles.

I carefully stuffed the duplicate of my lost treasure deep into the left front pocket of my dirt-encrusted Levis and sauntered home for supper, stroking the pearl handle with thumb and forefinger and reflecting on the mysteries of life.

Today, in retrospect, I can see that the answer lies in the country western grab bag of wisdom: "You gotta know when to hold 'em and know when to fold 'em." Or, as I might have put it at the age of 11, "You gotta know when to buy 'em and know when to cash 'em in; you gotta know who's the ultimate boss and know how to barter loss." For everything there's a time and a season—and even when there seems to be no reason, there is.

P.S. I kept my treasure in a White Owl cigar box buried under a stack of sweat socks in my closet. I used it to whittle wood carvings, slice strips of balsa wood for model planes, cut rope on bundled newspapers, and most of all to beat my brother George at mumblety-peg wherever and whenever I could talk him into a game. Never once did I get into a bloody street fight.

The Deed

It all took place on Deshong Alley in late August 1941. I remember because I was wearing George's old Wrangler overalls. I'd worn them to Larkin School that day because George had been gifted with a new pair for his birthday. (I'd helped Pop pick them from the pile stacked on a table in Montgomery Ward's). Anyway, George was sporting the new, and I was feeling my oats in his discards. His were bluer and stiffer; mine were fading and slightly frayed, but loose enough to allow knee-to-chin action, loose enough for sprints in my Joe Lapchick sneakers that imprinted tracks on the summer-soft, macadam-paved alley.

Deshong Alley was our Scheib Park for pick-up games, our dogleg of action, our direct trek to and from grammar school. Bert Redden lived and held court there, and we used his porch column as a marker for a double in our stickball games. Sylvester Wilson domiciled in a flat-faced, tired-eyed pre-Civil-War row house of disintegrating red brick, with warped window sills and a shredded screen door that allowed buzzing, green-eyed horseflies ready entry. But I digress.

It was the last of the seventh, and our tire ball games almost always ended after seven innings—sometimes sooner if Mom sent someone over to haul us away for supper. Paul Lukes was scratching the score that day, kneeling on one knicker-clad knee. Usually he used whatever marker was at hand—a stone, a brick chip— but today he was keeping score with a piece of chalk I'd swiped from Miss Ward's chalk box, which she kept on a narrow ledge above the coat hooks in the cloakroom. Little did that sweet lady know how often I'd dipped into that box in route to the boy's room in the basement. I routinely timed my raised-hand plea for relief about 15 minutes before morning recess just so I could "borrow" a few chalk strips.

I'll never forget the morning I leapt, tipped the box, and caught it just before it hit the floor. Facing into the coats, I slid the lid along the etched grooves, and— WHOA!—inside, along with the chalk sticks, there abided six confiscated penknives. Looking both ways for sudden entries into the cloakroom, I pocketed the needed chalk, then "borrowed" the pedigree of all pocketknives— a pearl-handled three-blader. What a tongue-biting find! I carried that beauty everywhere except into Pop's sightline. I practiced my mumbledy peg routine for months. George could never figure out why I was so hard to beat. Well, I'm spilling the truth now. Maybe it's part of this epic guilt I've slung around my neck like a dead albatross all these years.

Well, anyway, back to the stickball game. Paul Lukes was tending score. Our team was ahead four to three (two outs), bottom of the seventh. I was on the mound, and Billy Lykens had just pinged a weak rolling single. Buster Robinson ricocheted a double off Burt Redden's

Doric-columned porch, and my brother George was about to step to the chalk-marked plate in his new Wranglers.

Suddenly the summons to supper was upon us. Brother Dan slid the front door open (visible to me from my position on the mound), and he cupped his hands, hollering us home. We ignored him, so he descended the three granite steps to deliver the call in person. Two outs, two on, last of the seventh. Only George stood between a win for our side and a broken, unfinished game. Dan paused on the curb in front of Bowen's house, waiting for the trolley car to pass on its way into town. I sensed the game was about to slip away into the mosquito-infested twilight.

Quicker than a flash of light, an unthinkable plot hatched full-grown into my mind—a deed that proved evil was alive within me, waiting only for such a time as this to give birth to the unpardonable.

In the whimsical words of Dag Hammarskjöld, "When does one swim so far away from the shore that the point of no return is reached?" I was only 11 years old and in the kindergarten of street smarts, but I was still capable of massive blockage of conscience if presented with a Frank's Orange Nectar or a box of Walnettos. I could listen to Connie Lemko throttling out in his Ukrainian tenor all five stanzas of "Ship Ahoy" on a Sunday morning without my conscience ever recording a word of his pleadings.

Anyway, as twilight descended, as mosquitoes circled, as George stood there swinging his broomstick, brandishing all the intimidation he could muster and little knowing the plot I'd hatched, he suddenly dropped the stick and scooted nimbly over to the Eagle Café wall, slightly to the right of the screen door over which an illuminated sign proclaimed "LADIES' ENTRANCE." Stealthily, he leaned over and picked up the stickball bat I'd fashioned from an old rake and brought to the game

33

with me. How he knew it was there I'll never know.

I'd found the rake while junking behind Galey Hardware Store one day. They'd tossed it in the trash, and I'd swiped it along with about six cardboard boxes that I flattened and stacked on my wagon. The rake handle was split at the bottom, but my visionary eye saw its potential. I'd sawed the rake part off in the backyard while Sonny Lynch's German shepherd, Rinnie, growled at me through the slats in the fence between us. I could tell he was drooling to sink his teeth into my flesh, so I halted my work just long enough to finger a handful of stone-mingled dirt and whip it into his face. I barked in mocking falsetto as he took refuge behind the pear tree on the far side of the yard.

Anyway, I'd finished my bat-making routine by notching vertical slits into the end of the bat for distinction and set about taking practice swings with my new acquisition—gauging the weight, assessing my hand-eye coordination. But try as I might, that beautifully notched hickory stick was beyond my 11-year-old strength. But nonetheless I'd carried it to the game that day, hoping by surreptitious practice swings to elevate to an Elmer Valo, Sam Chapman, or Hank Majeski level.

So now here was George facing me down with my own bat. Dan hollered, and George turned to look at him—giving me the chance to make my move. I quickly reached into the frayed back pocket of his hand-me-down overalls and lifted out my "reserve," a concealed tire ball HALF THE SIZE of the sanctioned one in use. I fingered it into a Hal Newhauser forward backspin thrust and let loose with an air of superior finality, but instead of whiffing my perfect pitch George corked it as if it was delivered in slow motion.

His Ted Williams microsecond detection system gave his swing a brutal whip action, sizzling my unlawful-sized tire ball past my ear and generating the hum of 10,000 hornets in route to the honey farm. He corked a line drive so blinding it blurred as it sailed beyond the telephone pole midway up the dogleg alley, disappearing into the twilight somewhere beyond Eighth Street, beyond the chestnut trees on Larkin School grounds.

No one bothered to hunt it down. My side lost four to six, and we all left the scene for assorted suppers. I was the last to leave, kicking the curbstone near the cast-iron sewer cover in front of the Eagles Café as Patsy Logan leaned out the bay window above Miller's Bar and sassily said, "Who won the game, Davey?" The tables of my own underhanded behavior had been turned on me, and I was going home with a heavy heart. I ignored her, though I heard her loud and clear.

Joe Miller was spitting tobacco juice, arching it slightly beyond the curbstone, one foot folded at the knee, leaning against the window of his den of iniquity (Pop's name for his establishment) while he made small talk with George Patrycia, who was about to turn off his barber pole for the evening.

Though it seems unlikely now, it seemed to me then that everyone knew about the scam I'd pulled on George. Joe Quinn had a knowing look as he sat at ease on his stoop. Mr. Massi had just closed his parking lot and was walking home, taking methodical half-steps and avoiding my eye by pretending to look for coins in the gutter.

I walked back a few steps to pick up the chalk marker Paul Lukes had used to keep score and flung it across the street, hoping to hit one of the four cats sauntering slowly down our side alley, before mounting the front steps and walking the hallway to the kitchen where cold soup and a cold grilled cheese sandwich awaited me.

It's Friday ... Time to Levitate

Butterflies mingled in my stomach with an undigested peanut butter sandwich as I shuffled with the rest of my class to our seats, anxious for the Friday afternoon talent show to begin.

"Inspiration adds wings, but practice prepares," I mused, as I scanned the room for attitudes. The performers were listed on the blackboard in large, perfect cursive. I was happy to see my name listed last, right behind Tommy MacAlooso

Mrs. Ginter called the roll and then gave introductory remarks to quiet us down. A glance at the clock, hanging between framed prints of George Washington and Abe Lincoln, revealed it was 2:00.

All eyes followed Helen Koukedes, our first performer, as she walked confidently to the front of the classroom. All distractions ceased as Helen moved with perfect freedom across the scarred linoleum, twirling, leaping, and balancing on tiptoe in her pink ballerina slippers. Her ebony curls bounced wildly on squared shoulders as she pirouetted flawlessly.

Polite applause ushered Helen to her seat as Barney Massi lurched forward for his recital of the Gettysburg

Address. He was decked out in brown woolen knickers tucked slightly below his knees, the entire recitation was delivered in a flat monotone with hands interlocked behind his back. He finished with a sweeping gesture of his right arm and then headed for his seat in the rear. The sparse applause came mainly from his buddies Fred Parker and Aloysius McGrann, who, had they not shown approval, faced possible retribution on the playground. Barney was known for strong-arm tactics if he felt slighted. But, to his credit, he never beat up on the girls.

Reba Grange followed with a spirited a cappella rendition of "Columbia, the Gem of the Ocean," but she lost her audience when she fogged out on two crucial lines in the chorus. She attempted recovery by restarting from the beginning but drew a blank twice before throwing in the towel, walking dejectedly to her seat with an unfinished lyric drifting somewhere in the ocean of her memory. Her blonde curls drooped as if they shared her misery.

The sun slanted through clear windows as Tommy MacAlooso—hair plastered, grin confident—sauntered up the aisle, sensing he could sew it up. With a James Cagney flare, he adjusted his belt and then launched into his "Yankee Doodle Dandy" song and dance routine—a practiced performance with private lessons written all over it. His cleated shoes stomped the floor with alacrity, lifting chalk dust to shimmer in sun shafts. Sweat beads forming on his forehead, he danced until he dropped to one knee directly in front of Pat Nolan's desk and bellowed, "I am a Yankee Doodle boy!" Pat clapped so hard I thought her hands would bleed.

My spirit sagged. How could I follow that act, the sheer magnitude of all that talent, especially the MacAlooso finish? I felt limp. I could see by the clock that the bell would ring in 11 minutes, and the class— anxious to fly out the door—would pay little attention to my performance.

Mrs. Ginter spoke for a few minutes about the war bond drive, which gave me time to focus. As she droned on, I fingered my yo-yo in the palm of my hand with which I planned to orchestrate tricks I had practiced all week: "Walk the Doggie," a "Three-Leaf Clover," "Around the World," "Sleeping Beauty," "Shooting Star," then the finale of a series of complicated "Loop the Loops."

Mrs. Ginter finally intoned, "Last, among the performing artists—David Komarnicki."

As I stood facing the class, 25 pairs of eyes seemed to echo my sentiments, "Go ahead, Komarnicki, see if you can top MacAlooso."

Eyeballing the unconvinced, I searched for a look of approval, which I finally found in the encouraging smile of Mrs. Ginter.

Struck with a bolt of inspiration, I slipped the yo-yo off my right index finger, placed it my pocket, cleared my throat, then launched into a song I had memorized while listening to the jukebox in Charley Peck's Emporium.

Singing directly into Mrs. Ginter's confidence-inspiring eyes, I crooned,

This love of mine goes on and on,
Tho' life is empty since you have gone.
You're always on my mind, tho' out of sight.
It's lonesome thru the day,
But oh! the night!

A hush settled over the class. My confidence galloped like Hopalong Cassidy chasing the banditos. Then turning to despondent Reba Grange, I warbled,

39

I cry my heart out… it's bound to break.
Since nothing matters, let it break."
Then pivoting to Charlotte Hagy, I pleaded,
"I ask the sun and the moon,
The stars that shine . . .

Then zeroing in on Sally Ednak's face, with my arms extended, I delivered the probing question:

What's to become of it… this love of mine?

The thunderous response, especially from the girls, continued until the bell sounded. Mrs. Ginter, judging impartially by the applause meter, declared me the winner and awarded me the $.25 war bond stamp.

I sang to telephone poles and open windows all the way down Deshong Street that afternoon, until I reached my house. Pausing before the front window, I saluted the embroidered banner honoring Mickey, Johnny, Joe, Danny, and Richard—out there, somewhere, fighting the war.

P.S. a few months later, my swollen tonsils bloated my throat, so Dr. Gallagher dispatched them. And though I can't prove it, a full octave of my burgeoning baritone voice vanished along with them, aborting my latent Frank Sinatra career. I outgrew my yo-yo, but the reverential eyes of Sally Ednak still haunt me when lyrics of my chosen ballad cross my mind.

Big Sting Saturday

My sister Mary tells me I was a Thursday child, and how can I argue with someone who helped Doc Gallagher cut the cord? But if the day of birth imprints the psyche, I'd swear I entered the world on a Saturday. Saturday was the day my engine coupled on all the boxcars, crammed them full, and pulled them along the narrow-gauge tracks of childhood. In nostalgia's reveries, I see the rails running two miles east to Eddystone, four miles west to Marcus Hook, and two miles north to Chester Park, then stretching along the Delaware from the cattail rushes of Essington to the Chester-Bridgeport Ferry and beyond. The boxcars are filled with a random Barnum & Bailey collection of people and things (no neat, two-by-two arrangement like Noah's Ark).

Saturday was a trumpet with all the stops pulled out; it was a harmonica with nary a discord. Except, to be perfectly honest, for one—one particular Saturday that sticks to memory's walls like flypaper; one omen-filled Saturday that nearly derailed my train. That day has been sitting on the spur track of my mind for all these years, its ghosts crying out to be exorcised. But lest the memories run faster than my Joe Lapchick sneakers allow, I'll start where all Saturdays began:

41

1. A bowl of Wheaties.

2. Toasted Friehofer's bread spread thick with butter and grape jelly.

3. A glass of Ovaltine.

Thus energized, I made the three-and-a-half-block dash to the Washington Theater in an eyeblink. A dime gained me entry to a cowboy double feature, and I slotted a nickel into the candy machine for a box of Jujy Fruits. But this Saturday the box didn't drop. So I double-whacked the machine with both palms and— BINGO!!— down dropped two boxes. What a way to start the day!

Advancing to the second-row center, I proceeded for the next 90 minutes to soak up every move Buck Jones made as he lassoed and hogtied all criminals in Laredo. One box of Jujy Fruits consumed, I opened the bonus box and watched in awe as Hopalong Cassidy captured all rustlers and other assorted outlaws without aid of posse, gunplay, or mean-spirited words. When the theater lights came on, I loped toward the exit with the herd and resisted a sudden Silver-Screen-inspired urge to tackle the usher.

My squinting eyes greeted the high noon sun as I emerged to join the Market Street crowd. Turning north, I halted to watch a Goff's Seafood truck unload a galvanized tub of ice-packed, glassy-eyed flounder  for delivery to the Washington House (evil omen).

Crossing Fifth, I stepped nimbly and managed to avoid all sidewalk cracks until a Weinberg's hatbox knocked me into the plate-glass window of Spencer's Stationery Store. Down on one knee, I gazed up at a fashionably attired matron of huge proportions. With a glassy-eyed stare (reminiscent of the flounders I'd encountered up the street), she admonished me, "Watch where you're going, kid," and waddled up the street, hatbox still jutting out from her ample right hip. Good home training stifled my retort as I contemplated the sidewalk crack she'd made me step on (bad omen).

Regaining my footing, I sauntered down to the Pennsylvania Railroad's Sixth Street underpass, where the noon Wilmington-Baltimore-Washington Express had pulled in and was boarding passengers directly overhead. As I bent over to pick up a Lucky Strike wrapper, a steamy spray of soot, mingled with Pullman water closet extract, assaulted the back of my sweatshirt. The odor (which I have long since mentally classified with the time brother Dan locked me in our outhouse at 812 Upland Street) was overpowering. I shook my fist in vowed vengeance at the departing train and hustled home through the back-alley network.

My face turning purple, I held my breath until I reached the sanctuary of our household's cast iron bathtub. Once submerged, I double-scrubbed with Lifebuoy soap, soaking until the hot water turned cold. Toweling down, I double-checked for any lingering aroma, then slid into Levis and a freshly washed T-shirt.

Sliding my hand into my left front pocket yielded a skate key and a Popsicle stick branded "FREE" (good omen). Strapping on my skates, I headed for Charlie Peck's Ice Cream Emporium across the street, losing my footing for a moment as I crossed the tracks just a heartbeat ahead of the approaching trolley.

"You're cutting it close, kid!" the conductor bellowed, clanging the warning bell about 10 times.

I waved at the retreating trolley, laughing as I skated off to redeem the "FREE" stick gripped in my right fist. Unceremoniously entering Charlie's store, I slipped on the granite doorsill and ripped a hole in the lower left corner of the screen door. I skated nonchalantly onto the worn linoleum floor, as Charlie (not having seen the hole yet) hollered, "Close the screen door, Davey!" Turning, I complied—reflecting for a moment on how often Charlie had bellowed variations of that request.

Spring: "Shut the door, Davey—the rain, the rain."

Summer: "Shut the door, Davey—the flies, the flies."

Fall: "Shut the door, Davey—the wind, the wind."

Winter: "Shut the door, Davey—the cold, the cold."

Was I a slow learner or just deliberately provoking the limits of Charlie's tolerance?

I was fourth in line, waiting to cash in my freebie. As I waited, I watched Charlie dip his specialty: a Walk-Away Sundae made of one scoop of Breyer's vanilla served in a Dixie cup and topped with Hershey's chocolate syrup. A horseshoe of white hair framed his shiny bald pate at ear level, and his round specs magnified jolly Santa Claus eyes. He had a potbelly to match the Saint Nick image, and when his laughter was unleashed it sent earthquake tremors up and down the broad white apron draped around it.

His patience (which I tested almost daily) was legendary, and his neighborliness was boundless. Look at the countless times he'd rapped on our door to summon sister Vicky to his store telephone before we could afford our own. In wintertime Charlie would tirelessly shoulder a bag of "Blue" coal to our door so we could warm our bleak, cold kitchen. On special summer evenings, when my newspaper earnings allowed and peaches were in season, I'd ask Charlie to hand-pack a pint of peach ice cream. He knew it was Mom's delight, so he'd pack it tight and let some hang over the top. Then, handing it over the marble counter to me, he'd give me a knowing smile and say to my departing back, "Shut the door, Davey—the flies, the flies."

My turn, finally! I handed the Popsicle stick to Charlie. He eyeballed it, then whispered so the customers behind me wouldn't hear, "Are you sure this is yours, Davey? I don't see your name on it. Could this be the one your brother George was searching for under the booth yesterday?"

I smoothly sidestepped the question: "I'll take creamsicle this time, Mr. Peck."

Skating out, I closed the door without being reminded (hoping it would keep Charlie from noticing the hole in the screen). I sat on the warm cement steps next door, savoring every slurp and contemplating Charlie as a dispatcher of happiness to the neighborhood. As my tongue slipped the last layer of ice cream off the stick, I suddenly crowed, "Another winner! Another freebie!"— good omen.

Suddenly my tender conscience presented a cross-referenced catalog of budding criminality practiced by Joseph and Anna Komarnicki's eighth child on this neighborhood saint.

- Such as pitching pennies against his storefront in full view of all who passed by.

- Like repacking his punchboard with past winners, stuffing them in corner slots, knowing in advance I'd punch out a winner.

- Like rigging the pinball machine with wire from a coat hanger, sliding it into position to tap the bumpers and run up the score to register free games. (Buster Robinson tutored me on that ploy, and I'd play for hours without coughing up a nickel.)

- Like dropping enough slugs in the jukebox to memorize Frank Sinatra's crooning of "This Love of Mine."

45

- Like plastering juice-depleted wads of gum on the underside of his booths.

The litany was long enough to break me out in hives if I let my conscience continue speaking, so I silenced it and skated back to Charlie's store. Reentering, I skidded over to the soda fountain and perched on a stool. Whipping out my lucky stick, I grinned, "Another winner, Charlie. I'll take another creamsicle."

He stood erect, crossed his arms, and pinched the corners of his mouth with thumb and forefinger.

"How lucky can a kid get?" he finally said and dug for my reward in his over-frosted ice cream freezer. As Charlie stooped over, his bald head gave off a pink reflective glare, and I was suddenly overwhelmed with guilt for all my "Charlie violations."

So I decided to make penance by buying stuff. As Charlie handed over my second creamsicle of the morning, I blurted, "Mr. Peck, I want to buy the diamond-studded yo-yo in the window, the Dick Tracy cap gun, six rolls of caps, and two trick strings."

Emptying my pockets, I pushed the money toward him across the glass-topped candy case. Before taking it, Charlie rubbed his chin and gave me a proposition I couldn't refuse: "Davey, how would you like to earn back the money for what you just spent—and 50 cents besides if you do a good job?"

I was overwhelmed: "How?"

"Mow my lawn and rake up the clippings."

I didn't have to think twice: "Where's your house, Mr. Peck?"

"It's on 24th Street. Near Chester Park."

"You've got a deal, Mr. Peck," I said, stunned by my good fortune.

"Okay, Davey. The mower's in the backyard shed. Don't forget to take the yo-yo and cap gun with you."

Dropping my booty off at home, I wasted no time running the 17 blocks, moving faster than Hopalong's horse, Topper, at full gallop. As 90-plus degree heat barbecued me, I plowed that dull-bladed mower through Charlie's grass until water blisters broke on both thumbs.

Just as I cut the last strip, up the steep incline near the wrought iron fence, it happened: THE BADDEST OF BAD OMENS was unleashed on me. It was like a descending avenger for all I'd perpetrated on Charlie. Clipping the ground with the mower, I unearthed a subterranean compound of yellow jackets. They flew into formation, hovered, then headed for me as if I were a honeycomb farmer with a fresh crop.

With the black-and-yellow cloud following me, I flailed my way west on 24th Street, scraping against a thorny hedge as I turned south onto Edgmont. I thought of claiming sanctuary at First Presbyterian, but, as a Baptist on the lam, I wasn't sure they'd let me in.

As the dive-bombing yellow jackets propelled me past the Chester Rural Cemetery at 19th Street, two gravediggers leaning on long, flat-faced shovels gaped after me and then plunged back into their work as if they were preparing my final resting place. I remember the scene vividly, because it was just then that I felt two piercing stings just above my right kidney. Those avenging, renegade bees had made it inside my shirt and were going for my vital organs! As I reached Imschweiler's Funeral Parlor at 14th, a hearse with an open rear door seemed to beckon me. At 12th I shot across the B & O tracks without stopping, looking, or listening. At Deshong Park Art Museum the bronze lion wore a smirk that mocked my long overdue retribution.

The diehard battalion of bees buzzed me past Saint

47

Michael's Church until I reached the source of my stinging atonement: Charlie Peck's Ice Cream Emporium. I bypassed its pockmarked screen door and pummeled my way across the street to the refuge of home. Mom immediately whipped up her trademark cure-all: a secret-formula mix of mustard plaster, Epsom salts, boric acid, iodine, castor oil, and Ovaltine. I suffered in silence that night, biting on a towel while I slept fitfully.

Sunday morning I wobbled to church (staying home was not an option with Pop), took a front-row seat, and hunched forward to avoid seat contact. Through the narrowed slits of my swollen eyes, I watched young Pete Perozak—decked out in his perfectly creased white Navy uniform—take the pulpit. (It was his last Sunday before being shipped overseas). Pete solemnly opened the huge pulpit Bible, looked (so memory serves) straight toward me, and read: "God is not mocked. Whatever you sow that you shall also reap. Be sure your sins shall find you out."

After intoning these warnings, he turned slightly to the right, resting his left arm on the pulpit. In a muffled panic of disbelief, I leaned further forward to check out the circular patch on Pete's left sleeve.

I saw a giant yellow-and-black bee firing a machine gun. Pete Perozak had joined the Seabees: THE OMEN OF ALL OMENS! I toppled over, knocking down Danny Bartkow's trombone stand before I hit the floor. After the closing hymn, I streaked for the rear exit to avoid congregational comment.

My multifarious infractions on Charlie Peck henceforth ceased, and summer slid by without further chiding of conscience in that particular regard. (I did, however, use my new cap gun on night visitors from the Eagle Bar and Grill seeking

kidney relief in our narrow alleyway—an oft-repeated deed of which I am not proud. The diamond-studded yo-yo was used more nobly, as I captured the neighborhood championship).

School began after Labor Day, and summer sneakers gave way to high-tops laced just below my loose-banded knickers. I trudged up Deshong Alley to take my place (last in line) to await Mrs. Beacham's clanging of her miniature, handheld Liberty Bell. My mind—lost in summer reveries—snapped back to attention only when the infamous Wally Zabitka edged in front of me. We compared notes and spoke in muted tones of projected ways and means for good times. I could feel subtle shiftings in the resolutions made on Big Sting Saturday.

Mrs. Beacham's bell rang loud and clear. As I ascended the eight smooth, quarried steps leading to formal learning, I instinctively knew I had acquired a new mentor in dubious morality. But that's another story.

P.S. Charlie did pay me the extra 50 cents, even though I didn't stick around to rake up the clippings.

The Bike

Few shocks ever knotted my stomach with more pain than when I opened the back door to find my bicycle missing.

Paul and Jim were in the kitchen eating oatmeal, and unless they were pulling a gag, my bike was gone. Interrupting their consumption, I asked, "Did you guys see my bike?"

They shook their heads in negative unison and kept on spooning oatmeal. George was upstairs sleeping, having worked the night shift at the Boyd Diner, so what could he know?

Returning to the yard, I sat on a pile of firewood by the fence while Rinnie, Mrs. Lynch's German police dog slotted its muzzled fangs through the slats, drooling to take another chunk of my flesh. Rinny had already sampled my arm and rear end last year, and I guess the memory of the taste still lingered. Anyway, I threw a stump of wood at his exposed nose. Bull's-eye! He yelped and then retreated to the far side of the Lynches' yard, leaving me to fret over my own muzzled thoughts.

51

I sat there despondently, faulting myself for failing to haul my bike into the shed instead of leaving it in the yard all night.

I struggled to figure out who had the guts to creep down my narrow alley, open the squeaky gate, survey my yard, then wheel it away unseen.

My first suspect was Harvey. When I caught him creeping out of the yard with my shoeshine brushes last month, he confessed with a twang of remorse and a fake falsetto, "I'm sorry, Davey. All I can say is the Devil made me do it. It won't happen again."

A full moon lit the alley that night, and having seen *The Wolf Man* at the Mac Theatre and how the same moon had turned Lon Chaney into a killer wolf, I half believed the Devil could have put a whisper in Harvey's ear. Anyway, Harvey's police record was loaded with petty infractions, and one more moonlight caper might send him to Glen Mills Reformatory to join his cousin Sylvester.

"No, no, I won't panic," I told myself. "I'll just walk around town checking the neighborhoods before calling for outside help. "

I told Mom I was going for a walk—keeping quiet about my missing bike so as not to worry her. She asked me to run to Collins Grocery Store for a loaf of bread and some Campbell's soup. I was out and back in a flash, handing her the change, kissing her cheek, and then setting out on my heavy-hearted journey.

Not exactly sure where I was going, I flipped a coin, then headed for Harvey's house behind Massey's Parking Lot. Harvey's flat-faced row house was squeezed next to his cousin Doodle's, another prime suspect. Strolling nonchalantly down the narrow walkway behind their sheds, I peered over their improvised wooden fences but found no sign of my bike. I then walked up Saint Charles

Alley to Welsh Street, as alert as a squirrel on the prowl for acorns.

Merging onto Welsh Street, I stole a glance at the town clock a hundred yards away. It told me it wasn't quite nine—still plenty of time before my two o'clock swim practice at the Y.

Turning left I paused at the Tasty Doughnuts window to watch Joe, the owner, trigger batter into the circular grease container to fry a batch of fresh glazed doughnuts.

A disheveled old man stopped alongside me, eyeing the doughnuts as they turned a golden tan. His toothless jaw moved up and down as if he was actually chewing one. A sugary scent flowed through the ventilator, causing taste bud secretions so strong that I dug deep in my pockets for some change.

Finding a quarter amid the lint, I took a deep breath, grabbed the door handle, walked in, and called out, "Hi, Joe. Two fresh glazed, please. I'll wait for the ones in the hopper."

He pincered them out of the tank, cashiered the quarter, then handed me 15 cents along with the doughnuts and a warm thank you.

I walked out with one between my teeth, the other in the bag. Feeling a sudden flush of magnanimity, I handed the bag to Mr. Hard Times. "Sir, could you please eat this? I forgot I'm on a diet and bought one too many."

He smiled, revealing his toothless gums, and before he could speak I scooted towards Sixth Street, where I paused to scan the next four blocks for any sign of my bike.

I saw nothing but locals and a line of Yellow Cabs at the railroad station, so I decided to walk through the tunnel beneath the east and westbound tracks.

Entering the tunnel, I belted out, *"Give me land, lots of land, under starry skies above. Don't fence me in."* For that brief moment, the sugar coating lingering on my taste buds and the explosive lyric reverberating in my eardrums teamed up to energize my sagging spirit.

Emerging into the main lobby of the station, I headed over to the payphones and checked the slots for returned coins. No luck. Further malingering was squelched when I caught the roaming eye of the railroad detective. He'd had me cataloged in his list of questionables for some time, so I made a hasty exit through the swinging doors and headed up Market Street toward the river.

Gauging the traffic flow, I sliced across Market Street to Kresge's Five and Dime, entered, then walked over to the lead soldier display counter, where I immediately noticed they'd added lead molding kits.

"WOW! I could mold my own army," I thought.

While reading the instructions on how to pore the lead into the mold, it suddenly struck me that in a "full-moon moment" on my last visit I had pocketed (borrowed) two lead soldiers. Like Harvey I wanted to fault the Devil, but my home training wouldn't allow it.

While standing there biting my lip, I heard a gentle voice, "Can I help you, sonny?"

Raising my guilt-flushed face, I stammered, "No, thank you, ma'am, I've already helped myself ... I mean, I was just looking to buy the mold-your-own-kit but I forgot my money, so I'll have to come back later."

"That's all right, son, we've got plenty more in the backroom, so don't you rush home and get hit by a car."

I shuffled out of the store feeling I ought to run home and grab the two purloined soldiers from my cigar box, but returning them might be trickier than "borrowing"

54

them in the first place. Anyway, the street noise and sidewalk congestion snapped me back to my purpose, which was to find my bike.

While I stood curbside waiting for passage rights at Fifth Street, a fat man approached and settled his bulk beside me. When the light flicked green, I stood motionless, watching this huge specimen of humanity waddle his way across the street. Each forward thrust took consideration of the protruding belly, maneuvering around it with a curiously splayed gait. First his heel touched down, and then his toes followed on a 45-degree angle. His rigid spine strained backwards to counterbalance the extension of his paunch. As he negotiated the opposite curb after crossing, shoppers cut a wide swath in deference to his imminent approach.

I froze in awed wonderment, pondering how many meals had to be chewed, swallowed, and stored for a stomach to balloon forth in such defiance of gravity. The food alone, if ingested at the Boyd Diner on Blue Plate Specials at 35 cents apiece, would cost at least $1,000 in cold cash, not to mention the tips. Marveling at the frontal immensity, the determined movement of Mr. Epicure, I backed up and leaned on a parking meter, locked in philosophic consideration of cause and effect. I wondered whether I could ever eat my way across the habit-of-no-return and bloat into the *Guinness Book of Records* by scarfing down 50,000 Medford hot dogs at Texas Wieners or attacking a 90-foot hoagie at Stackey's. The answer to this mathematical conundrum did not materialize, so I crossed Fifth Street on the next green.

At the Colonial Courthouse, I glanced across to the Washington Theatre marquee and grumbled to myself, "Some cotton picker stole my bike and caused me to miss Tom Mix and Buck Rodgers today. The louse could be sitting in there right now, enjoying a box of Goobers and watching the movie while I'm scouting the city to find him. The rat—if it happened to him, he wouldn't like it any more than I do."

Just think, I'd traded my official Bill Dickey mitt and a stack of hard-earned quarters for the bike. And that wasn't all—the glove was a gift from brother Mickey. His scribbled V-mail told me his Army unit had to dump the sports stuff, so instead of tossing it all, he sent me the glove. It arrived just in time for Christmas. I slept with it under my pillow for two weeks and thought it was the best gift ever. Then Eddie offered me his Schwinn with the whitewall tires for the glove.

Well, knowing Mickey and how feisty he was about a good deal, I knew he'd approve, so I shook hands on it right there. I didn't have the money on me, so Eddie rode me home on the crossbar. I bolted upstairs, lifted the money from my cigar box, returned, and handed him the glove with the quarters in the palm, piled right next to Bill Dickey's signature.

But that was then, and this was now. I brought myself out of my reverie and immediately tripped over the foot of a dapper man about to enter the Delaware County National Bank with two other distinguished gents. Before my face hit the ground, two outstretched arms caught my shoulders.

"Careful, young fella," my rescuer said with a smile.

The smile belonged to the face of none other than John McClure. The foot I'd tripped over belonged to J. Howard Pew, the president of the bank. His face had been etched in my memory ever since last July when he shook my hand in congratulations for depositing $2 in my newly opened Christmas Club account at his bank. The third kindly face belonged to Tom McCabe, president of Scott Paper Company.

"I'm sorry, gentlemen," I mumbled apologetically.

"No harm done," Mr. Pew chuckled, with a gleam in his bespectacled eyes.

"I was checking to see what I missed today at the theatre, and I didn't look where I was going," I explained. "Sorry."

"You don't have to apologize, son," said Mr. McClure. "But tell me, why are you going to miss the movies today?"

"Well, uh … I, I have to run an all-day errand, and that's more important."

"Now son, since you run errands, and you're willing to take your Saturday to do that, why don't you drop by my office next Monday after school and we'll talk about running errands for me. My office is in the corner building across the street and I'm on the eighth floor. Here's my card."

I glanced at the card and then said "Thank you, Mr. McClure, I will, I will!"

They all smiled as I walked away backwards, waving until they disappeared into the bank.

"Well, Dave," I thought to myself, "you never can tell what can come from tripping over a caring foot."

Just then the traffic light flicked green, and so I sauntered across the intersection on my way to Third Street, still thinking about my good fortune in the job prospects department. The trolley bell, signaling passenger offloading at Third and Market, snapped me back to the present.

Mr. Baker, a good friend of Pop's, was hobbling around the corner, talking with a man who had no doubt seen better times. Mr. Baker has a clubfoot, and he wears a shoe with a heel the size of my clenched fist. Each step he takes is an act of faith. His voice carries the clarity of a bullhorn, and his smile warms like the noonday sun.

They're heading toward the Union Gospel Mission where Mr. Baker runs the operation.

Not long ago, I had sat with Pop in the back row of the mission's chapel, looking at row upon row of stoop-shouldered men. Their attendance at the gospel service was a must if they were to enjoy a meal and a bed. A wall banner hung behind the pulpit, declaring, "JESUS SAVES," and the bible verse John 3:16 was posted to its right.

Observing the men from my angled view in the rear, I listened as Mr. Baker declared, in plain talk, how much God loved them and what they must do to make things right. If his plea had any effect, it wasn't obvious to me. A blanket of collective body heat was trapped in the overcrowded room, and my quivering nose was aware that a hot shower by all would clear the air. While I listened to all the muffled coughs from heavily congested bronchials and watched unshaven jaws yawn in slow motion, Pop sat upright, nodding agreement with Mr. Baker's sermon, which for him shone as true as a lighthouse beam.

The Market Square was alive with Saturday's theatrics. It was Chester's only square, and much of the flow of city life intersected here. So I just stood curbside, leaning on a splintered pole, observing people parading by:

- A shuffler with rundown heels.

- A portly lady with a drooping hemline.

- A middle-aged black man with bowed legs.

- A pigeon-toed kid, sporting my favorites, a pair of Joe Lapchick sneakers.

- An old-timer, whose arthritic hip provoked a grimace of swallowed pain.

- An angle-walker who kept running into people.

- A mince-stepper, moving to some internal tune I couldn't identify.

- An arm-swinger with a military look in his eye.

- A woman wearing open-toed patent leather shoes and sporting a noticeable bunion,

And, ah, here came the sure step of Officer Lykens walking his beat, the gentlest purveyor of controlled force ever to patrol the city—and, yes, the father of my playmate Billy.

Market Square ran a straight line to the river three blocks away. The square was where the trolley terminated and then returned to Philly. It was the home of Stotter's, Chester's largest department store, where Santa was presented every Christmas. The Union Gospel Mission offered a haven for the down-and-out, and Bethel Court offered solace for sailors who strayed from the straight and narrow. Third-rate restaurants stood shoulder to shoulder. Sapovitz Jewelry offered diamond rings on credit for two bucks a week, and Lou's Pawn Shop eased a need till payday.

Market Square had hotel bars that offered beds upstairs for hangovers or a cab to get you home. Saint Paul's Cemetery welcomed future patrons to ponder life's brevity, and Wang's Laundry starched collars and cuffs for bachelors.

There was a deli for the kosher folks, a Pentecostal church for the fervent in faith, and streetwalkers announcing their trade with roaming eyes. The Salvation Army band convened here on Friday evenings, piercing the air with their ponderable rendition of "Are You Washed in the Blood of the Lamb?" Commission Row, a block away, featured hefty-breasted chickens and ice-packed walleye.

Yes, Market Square was where Chester's high tide

intersected with the low, where the World, the Flesh, and the Devil duked it out with spirit-filled sermons and Salvation Army brass. And here I was—standing ringside at Stotter's corner, ready to duke it out with the twerp who pilfered my bike.

A trolley on the turnaround was being eased 180 degrees, pushed by two blue-uniformed conductors, while the queued crowd waited to board for all points north.

Someday I was going to pay my fare to ride it to the end of the line and, with camera-ready eyes, click all stops along the way. I'd sit in a backseat watching patrons board and checking where they got off. I'd take note of their faces, their gait, whether they were stiff or friendly when they sat. I'd note if they were buried in the local newspaper or gazing out the window. And I'd mimic the conductor, calling out each stop in its turn whether he enjoyed his job or was just along for the ride and the paycheck.

Suddenly I flashed back to last winter's blizzard, when Chester's pavements were buried in snow so deep I'd made a bundle shoveling it.

It had been just about dusk when I'd crouched between parked cars, waiting as the trolley rolled slowly into town. Lurching out, I'd belly-flopped my sled, grabbed the rear of the trolley, and felt the spray of the trolley wheels rolling over crusted snow packed in the groove of the track. It had been a smooth ride till a dry patch had jerked my sled from under me. I'd scraped along on my wool jacket, holding tight to the rear bar of the trolley till I'd finally let go. Scrambling to the curbstone, I'd sat for a long time, glad that I'd hitched the ride, because it gave me bragging rights. But I was still grateful I wasn't terminated for my impulse.

A passing paddy wagon whiplashed me back into focus, as it sped across Market Square heading for the police station. I craned my neck to catch who was getting a ride to the slammer.

A Yellow Cab pulled curbside, stopping directly in front of my foot, causing me to step back. A mannequin-thin man, draped in a camel's hair coat, bolted out, handed the cabbie a couple of bills, called "Keep the change" over his shoulder, and trotted into Stotter's Department Store.

I felt dwarfed by my search. I knew I had to keep going, but the odds of seeing my bike again were slimmer than solving a *Philadelphia Inquirer* crossword puzzle. And what if I did spot the lout with my stolen goods? Could I catch him before he got away?

Deciding to continue, I crossed Market Street and passed by Saint Paul's where John Morton, whose signature was inked on the Declaration of Independence, lay buried.

I wondered whether John Morton ever had his bike stolen when he was a kid. When Quakers caught a thief, they put him in stocks right here in this public square. All his friends laughed at him, gave him the raspberries, cupped their hands and called him what he was: A THIEF. Imagine the shame his parents had to deal with, having a lousy, low-down, bike-stealing son displayed in the public square, while they were kneeling in Saint Paul's on Sunday morning praying for him. I was glad I wasn't born in John Morton's time, or I'd be in the graveyard with him right now. No, I'd rather be looking around town for my bike.

I'd walked to the river many times to ride the Wilson Line to Riverview Beach. It was a special treat to walk the gangway, hand the ticket over, run to the rail and scan the far-off Philadelphia skyline, then turn to watch the wide sweep of the gray tide as it carried us along towards Wilmington.

61

Those rides taught me more about freedom than reading about Paul Revere, Bunker Hill and all the pictures plastered in Miss Fenton's room in Larkin School. A brown bag full of bologna sandwiches, chocolate Tastykakes, some pretzel sticks, and a dollar for the bumper cars, the Ferris wheel, and the roller coaster. Ah, Saturdays were made for rolling on the river or riding a bike, but today I had neither, only memories and a regret I was hoping to heal.

I walked toward the river more for the view than for hope of bagging the thief. To stay focused I took inventory. As I passed the Full Gospel Tabernacle (a name Pop would heartily approve of), I glanced across the street and noticed five houses in a row with the downstairs converted to lunchrooms or restaurants. What a lineup of food troughs leading to Scott Paper Company! With thousands of workers passing every day, some of them were bound to stop for a sandwich, coffee, or a bowl of soup. And on slow days the owners could always eat the leftovers, take it right upstairs where they lived, and feed the family.

Doubling my pace as I approached the dock, I stretched my neck to check out the picture painted on the water tower high above the roof of the great toilet paper enterprise. It was hard to believe that every bathroom in the Western world smiled with gratitude for Scott's 1,000-sheet roll of soft tissue.

Walking to the dock, I watched as a steel barge, piled high with wire-wrapped paper bales, was being offloaded by a crane. The bales were hoisted onto conveyors belts, then disappeared into the cavernous warehouse.

I gawked like a tourist until a river rat the size of a raccoon began a slow crawl towards me along the top of the cement retaining wall. Stomping my foot, I belted a note two octaves above middle C, and that fat rat, trying a U-turn, belly-flopped into the oil-slick river. This incident killed my interest in paper-processing, so I cut out for the Wilson Excursion Line boarding area to stand among the crowd waiting for the boat's arrival. Leaning on the guard rail, I surveyed the flat tree-lined New Jersey shoreline through squinting eyes. The wind let it be known it was November, but the sun shone as clear as an eagle's eye. A Coast Guard boat trolled toward Philadelphia, patrolling the vital war-primed shoreline.

I gazed downriver, watching wind-slanted smoke billow from factory stacks. Baldt Anchor, Philadelphia Electric, Ford Motors, Sinclair, Sun Oil—all broad-shouldered their spots facing the Delaware River. Looking towards Philadelphia, I spotted cranes like giant praying mantises, lowering steel plates into place to be formed into welded cargo tankers at Sun Shipyard. My brother John had worked among them before the war.

I thought of summer days at the Jersey Shore, where families flocked to the beaches, the parents lying around on blankets while the kids inner-tubed the waves and stayed afloat till their fingers shrank from waterlog. Right now, I was looking at a sandless beach on the Delaware River, where parents worked at assembly lines for fifty weeks so they could take their kids to the Jersey Shore for two.

All this surveying of streets and river scenes was not helping me find the culprit who rode off with my bike. Better retrace my steps and get on with it.

Walking back the way I came, I reentered Market Square, then paused by the Wolf Building to decide which way to go—west or east? After mulling it over, I decided not to walk west, because West End kids stayed in their own neighborhoods. And the West Side was loaded with Italians and Slavs, neither of which were ethnically disposed toward bike stealing. Most Italians were rich enough to get every kid in the family a bike, and the Poles and Ukes would hang their kid upside down till he was

63

blue in the face for stealing and bringing shame on the family. No, it had to be some louse from my own end of town whose greedy eye had spotted me riding around. So I trotted east on Third, deciding to check all streets and alleys all the way to Morton Avenue.

Puffy gray clouds were moving in from Philly— sort of the way I felt, puffy and gray with anger. Walking Third to Welsh along the graveyard, I decided to hop the low wall and meander among the graves. Most markers, lashed by centuries of wind and rain, couldn't be read even close up, but among the few I could, I discovered that death struck when some were very young:

Mamie A. Chestnut, born in June 1859, died in August 1860.

Althea Perkins, born December 28, 1853, died February 1, 1854.

Joshua Eyre lived only nine months.

Ann Jane Newlin died when she was 12.

It was sad that kids younger than me were buried here. Maybe they died from fever, whooping cough, the mumps, chickenpox; maybe they were run over by a horse. Who knows? Doesn't say—just these fading records of their names, their birth and death, and a chiseled Scripture promise of eternal hope beyond the grave.

I felt vulnerable as I continued on my way. I could die today, I thought, or tomorrow I might get hit by a car. Memory blinked me back: I could have died from swollen tonsils that closed my throat a year ago. "Thanks, Dr. Gallagher, for slicing them out," I whispered to myself. "Someday if I have a son, I'll name him after you."

And what about last winter when, streaking down Crosby Street hill, I couldn't stop my sled from ramming into the front tire of a car? What a close call that was, my head right there beside the front wheel of a black sedan, a hubcap spelling "FORD" staring me in the face.

When I grow up, if I live till then, I'll buy a Ford in gratitude for their good brakes. Yes, life's as pockmarked as a horse thief's career in a Buck Jones movie. You never know when you're going to end up on Boot Hill.

Leaping the graveyard wall at Crosby Street, I looked north, and the scene made me gulp so hard my throat gagged. The wooden sign along the porch of the second house from the corner read, "**THE JUVENILE COURTHOUSE AND DETENTION HOME.**" This triggered a memory montage of infractions that qualified me for a long stretch of free room and board:

- Fighting in the alley with Sylvester (currently in their care for hookying school).

- Getting caught swimming in the Leiper Quarry on school time.

- Being seen running from Mrs. Strayhorn's house, as she stomped on burning manure-filled bags placed there on Mischief Night.

- Smashing the Yellow Cab neon sign with a wad of rope-wrapped paper while playing Take It or Leave It (Bobbie Berman covered that infraction).

- Leaving my house while the quarantine sign was still posted in the window.

- And a for-sure time (if I'd been caught), when I knocked the railroad detective's Stetson off his head with an ice-packed snowball.

Rather than keep on gawking at the wide-porched house where I would have been tanked till the court turned me over to the Glen Mills Reformatory (visitors allowed two to five on Saturdays), I decided Crosby was a bad omen and tripped my way west on Third. As I made my way over the tree-displaced, red brick sidewalk, I

65

thought about my history of shady behavior and remembered Pop's oft-repeated warning, "Be sure thy sins shall find thee out."

Trying to put these doom-packed thoughts out of my mind, I counted houses while walking along—twenty-six porchless homes in a row, each with three limestone steps. The sidewalk and curbs were cleanly swept, and the old knotted trees (surviving since Civil War times), afforded shade and softened the street noise just six feet from their front windows. Same set-up as my house, I thought, but we had no trees on Seventh Street.

As I balance-beamed myself along the curb, I saw the sun slanting on silver in the gutter. I stopped, scooped a finger in the cindered dirt, and—Whoa!—a quarter just lying there, waiting for a gutter-seasoned eye. My eye was in the gutter all the way to Madison, checking the inventory of curbside discards: Baby Ruth and spearmint gum wrappers, a Pepsi bottle cap, a broken shoelace, coal lumps that didn't make it down the cellar chute on delivery day, a welder's glove, horse manure, stray dog discards, a kickable oilcan, brown lunch bags, a skate key (which I pocketed), popsicle sticks, and a Pabst Blue Ribbon beer coaster.

Reaching Madison I gazed out toward the river, where the huge Downham Press building ran the length of the block. "Why did I come this way?" I wondered. "Not many houses, no real neighborhood, and not much chance of finding the crook who made off with my bike."

I trudged on till I reached Morton Avenue, where Sun Shipyard sat like a cavernous mouth on the Delaware. Its well-guarded gate swallowed up 10,000 moms and dads every day, then belched them out eight hours later—a little richer, a little happier, knowing that their welds and rivets seamed ships that carried the cargo needed to win the war.

How many times I'd watched my brother John leave our house for work at the shipyard before he joined the Navy. I'd watched as Mom handed him thermos and lunchbox and received a kiss on the forehead in return, and one morning I decided to tag along with him just for the fun of it. His long legs vaulted the steps and made me half-run to keep up. We turned Crosby corner, passed the Chester Rescue Mission and Smedley's Junk Shop, then turned left on Sixth. We chewed the fat all the way to Morton Avenue, turned beneath the Pennsylvania Railroad tracks, passed the Sylvan Diner at Third Street, then paused as the shipyard gates came into view.

"Thanks for the company, Davey," John said, patting me on the head and flipping a quarter into my upturned palm. I watched him with brotherly pride as he disappeared among the press of men, ready to work another day for all that a paycheck brings.

Johnny was ten before I came along. He learned to crawl, walk, and run during the Roaring Twenties, and when the Depression came along he fast became a plus on the ledger of family income. He learned at a young age how to earn money doing whatever willing feet and hands could do.

Our bond was forged early on, because one way he helped Mom out was by carting me around when I was too young to navigate on my own. And when I was out of diapers and old enough to do my business in the family outhouse, he'd carry me out on cold winter evenings and stand shivering by the rickety wooden door while I obeyed nature's call. Ever since, I've held him as my hero.

Johnny was born on American Street in Philly, along with Mickey, Mary, and Vicky. The family then moved to Lester, where Joe was born, then on to Chester, where five more were added to the clan. We weathered the knocks of seven landlords before taking on a mortgage.

Johnny was the one who warned me about the gypsies that drove their horse wagon through the neighborhood, bellowing, "Any old rags? Any old rags?" He told me they'd kidnap me if I gave them a chance, so I ran for safety every time I saw them.

Mickey, Johnny, and brother Joe laid the groundwork for neighborhood respect and all the other stuff that mattered most to a kid, mainly how to step lively through the cageless zoo of Chester without letting the animals eat you alive. Some tried, but they never got more than a fist in their mouth, usually delivered by one of my older brothers.

"So many streets to choose from," I thought, as I stood motionless under the railroad track overpass on Morton Avenue, pondering my next move. Street noise, mingling with the roar of an overhead freight train and the belched fumes of truck traffic, urged me along to North Street a short block away.

There were a bunch of kids playing stickball out in the street, but they weren't looking for another player, especially a kid who didn't live on the block. They halted the game long enough to check me out as I moved through, and I recognized Bobbie Smith standing on the manhole cover used as the pitching mound. I gave him a wave as I moved on to resume my search on Potter Street.

At Eighth and Potter I ducked into Clark's corner store to spend 15 cents on a creamsicle, five war card gum packs, and a Mounds Bar. I kibitzed with my buddy Shadow, with whom I often swam in the Leiper Quarry. Shadow wouldn't win Mom over if I brought him home for meatloaf on Sunday, but we got along great and I could trust him, so when I told him what I was up to, he said he'd keep an eye out.

Heading toward Ninth, I paused to look up Congress Alley, where a crap game was in session near the fence three houses up the alley. About twelve kids were standing in horseshoe formation as Pete Favario shook the dice alongside his right ear and hollered out incantations: "Seven come eleven, either one, dice, either one."

I walked closer to add an appendage to my street education. Pete had a hot hand and rolled three straight passes as I stood there in wonderment at his power over the dice. The money to cover the bet was tossed in a pile on the ground. Pete intoned his fervent commands for good luck, and— Bingo!—another seven.

The game became heated with street talk: "Lemme look at the dice, are they loaded?" Sam Cook yelled. "You can't keep it up, you lucky ginzo. I'll cover the whole pot!"

Pete was big enough to whip anybody in the alley but good-natured enough to laugh off the friendly slur. He just stood there tweaking the dice in his right hand until all the money settled in the dust.

After six straight passes Pete still held the dice, so I backed up to get on with my pursuit. "Six straight passes and letting the pot ride. That's enough money to walk into Stotter's and buy two bikes," I thought.

I crossed at Ninth Street, where the Third Presbyterian Church covered half a block, and spotted Reverend Lance Latham stepping out of the manse. This venerable pastor of the most architecturally beautiful church in Chester was a silver-haired prince of the pulpit, and his Summer Bible School filled a warehouse with kids every year. I myself was one of the tadpoles caught in the fishnet cast by the parental network of Chester every July.

I was starting to get discouraged, aware that time was running out. I hurried on toward 10th Street, where I saw little Ed Kuhlman pulling his red wagon, stacked with one-gallon water jugs packed to fit perfectly between wooden dividers that kept them from rattling or breaking. I was used to seeing little Eddie hauling his load home up Melrose Hill, pulling with all his might up that two-block incline that tested a kid's will for all it was worth. And his wagon load was worth about 40 cents C.O.D., which went a long way toward putting food on the table for his family.

Turning onto 10th, I spotted a couple of kids on bikes right in front of the house where I'd been born twelve years before. I have no actual memory of my debut on the second floor, but I got all the details from my sister Mary, and, if asked, I could give a ten-minute talk on how the family welcomed me back then. In the years since, my older brothers had developed a crazy way of showing they still felt the same way.

Making a left onto Edgmont Avenue, I was met by the imposing sight of the Deshong Art Gallery, standing alone on a low rise guarded by two pedestaled lions. A sense of awe washed over me as I paused to focus on the wonder of its pure white marble glory, the wonder of where Mr. Deshong got all the money to build this edifice and then fill it with so many paintings. And what a beautiful park he gave to kids, kids like me who raided the seckel pear trees every summer. I hoped someday I could do the same for kids I didn't know.

As I angled through the Larkin playground toward Deshong Alley, I had a strong hunch that the thief had noticed me riding around this very same playground the day before, then followed me home and saw me walk my bike down the narrow alleyway to my yard.

Since I no longer had a bike for a lowdown thief to snatch, I didn't have to worry about being followed today. I could tell by the sun that it was time to head home and get ready for swim practice, so I hot-footed it the next two blocks. I announced my arrival to Mom, made a baloney sandwich and ate it in route to my room, where I lifted a quarter from my cigar box, then grabbed the YMCA towel I'd borrowed on my last visit.

From my first dive into the chlorine-treated pool, my churning anger started to fade. I felt relaxed enough to realize I still had a strong body and a clear mind, and that rotten things happened. I still hungered to learn all I could about the world around me, learn about who I was, where I fit in, what was important to my family, what I could learn from my brothers to help me swim through the high tides without drifting sideways into serious trouble. It would be so easy to just start drifting into gang stuff and forget the things Mom and Pop and my older brothers tried to warn me about.

After swim practice, I talked with Eddie Morrell, my coach, and told him about my stolen bike. Eddie had a magical way of making me feel things would turn out okay, and so I left the Y in a positive mood.

On my way home I took my quarter to Charlie Peck's Store and spent it all on a Pepsi, a double-dipped chocolate cone, a Milky Way, and five chewy caramels. I then sat in a booth listening to the jukebox, licking and chewing, while Bing Crosby warbled, *"I'm dreaming of a white Christmas."*

The rest of Saturday was spent serving my paper route. I was feeling a little tired when I got back home, so I retreated to my room to catch up on my reading: a stack of Captain Marvel and Spider Man comic books.

Sunday started with its usual cycle: breakfast, church, and then home. Rather than sit around moping about my bike, I decided to resume my search by walking through Sun Village, armed with a Kodak shot of my missing bike. I started my canvass on McDowell, then moved on to Elsinore Street, where I stopped to talk to Art Nazigian sitting on his porch. I then decided to walk every street in the village, beginning with Baldwin. I did a lot of walking, a lot of waving at kids I knew from school, and a lot of showing of my bike picture.

I managed to enlarge the network of eyes on the lookout, but after two hours of walking and talking I left the village clueless and decided to walk west on 12th Street along the B & O Railroad.

I reached Potter Street as the crossbar dropped, halting traffic while a freight train rolled by. Boxcars painted with strange-sounding names were coupled together on this leg of their journey but destined for different tracks on down the line. I watched and counted the cars with thoughts that someday I'd ride the rails to Baltimore, to Ohio, maybe all the way to Santa Fe.

I quit counting the rolling boxcars when I reached 137 (a new record), then walked to Congress Alley, where I kicked pebbles and stones while checking the content of yards all the way to Crosby Street. The stuff I saw, the junk people kept, made me realize how strong a grip the Depression still held on people: dilapidated wagons loaded with plants in cracked pots, rusted bedsprings, piles of rotted wood. Clotheslines crisscrossed the yards, air-drying sheets, socks, shorts, overalls, kids' knickers, blue shipyard shirts—all that a heavy-duty Maytag would hold if the work-weary moms could afford one.

Tired, hungry, and empty of hope, I emerged at Crosby Street, then dolefully walked down Deshong Alley to home, where Mom fixed me a huge bowl of pot roast (heavy on the gravy) mingled with sweet carrots, peas, chopped potatoes, onions, celery, and broccoli. I ate my way right out of my grief and was so grateful that I volunteered to wash the dishes.

I decided to spend the evening in the living room with my younger brothers, Paul and Jimmy, reading the funnies and listening to *The Shadow, Inner Sanctum*, and *The Johnson Family* on the radio.

Before I got to the funnies, I saw *Inquirer* headlines announcing the sinking of the *USS Juneau*. The five Sullivan brothers went down with the ship, and Walt Seigle who lived around the corner on Crosby Street was among those lost at sea with them.

I'd seen Walt just a few months ago, turning Crosby Street corner. I'd waved as he crossed to enter Charley Peck's, then exited with an ice cream cone, heading into town. I'd watched him play stickball in front of his house with Buster Robinson, the Wilson brothers, and Paul Lukes or swim in Chester Creek with my brothers. I'd watched him light the fuse of a cherry bomb, then slide it under a tin can in his alley on the Fourth of July. I'd noticed him in Tucker's Pool Room, sitting in a penknife-initialed captain's chair, watching Jackie Kerrigan pace around the front table intent on running the rack in a nine-ball game.

Neighborhood life had changed suddenly when we got into the war. Embroidered stars appeared in front windows up and down the block: gold when someone was killed in action, silver when they were wounded, and blue when they were still in service. Five stars hung in our window when Mickey, Johnny, Joe, Dan, and our sister Vicky's husband, Richard, joined up.

The Japs sneaked up on us at Pearl Harbor, Roosevelt gave a speech, war was declared, and the local draft board started assigning numbers. Walt was one of those who decided not to wait for his number to be called. He aced his physical, endured basic training, was assigned to the *Juneau* and before long was standing on the deck bursting with the zeal of life, proud to be doing his part in the war.

* * *

"Will I make it home to marry Sally?" he wonders one day as he climbs the steel steps up to the

ship's galley. "Will we have as many kids as my mom and dad?"

Then a torpedo blasts a hole the size of his house in the Juneau's *bow. The ship begins to list, then splits in half as he frantically climbs the ladder for a way up and out. The taste of saltwater sweeps over his tongue as the sea pulls him into its swirling embrace.*

As he sinks, his mind whispers, "Goodbye, Mom; goodbye, Pop; goodbye, Sally. I love you."

Floundering in the murky water, his chest bursting for air, his mind embraces a verse oft repeated in Sunday school: "For God so loved the world that he gave his only Son, that whoever believes ...." His eyes close as his body sinks with his shipmates to a hero's grave, but his spirit rises to eternal life.

I went to bed early, thinking about the Seigle family and the vacant chair at their supper table, about his girlfriend and the kids they'd never have.

Monday at school I feigned attentiveness, but my mind was a vacant lot. After school I walked home a different route, down Upland Street to Seventh, still hoping I'd see my bike. No luck. After an early supper, I decided to go sit in the Crozer Library on Ninth Street and dig into the World Book for a project Mrs. Eachus had given me.

I left the house, full of food but empty in spirit as I walked slowly up Deshong Alley. When I stepped onto the Larkin School playground, I spotted a bike leaning against the chestnut tree by the ash pile. Kids were shooting marbles by the side of the school about 30 feet away. I sauntered over to the bike, read the label on the frame, and got a feeling of confused recognition. It was a Schwinn all right, but the tires weren't the same and the

74

fenders were painted pale green (the color of my stomach bile the day I was so sick I threw up in the galvanized bucket Mom placed next to my bed).

I walked over, grabbed the handlebars, flipped the bike upside down, checked the frame near the crossbar— and, sure enough, there was my mark, a "K" I carved into the frame with my penknife. I learned this from watching a cowboy movie where the owner of the K Corral branded all his cattle with a "K."

I felt like shouting, "Shazam!," but I muffled it. I looked over at the marble crowd and decided to wait around to see who claimed the bike. While waiting, I started a chestnut and acorn collection from tree droppings. Moving around like a squirrel, I piled them near the tree trunk where I decided to sit until the marble game ended.

They played till dusk, and finally an unfamiliar face walked toward the bike. I waited till he was 4 feet away, then said loudly, "Is that your bike?"

He turned, looked at me, then said, "Who are you? What's it to you?"

I increased my volume: "I'm Dave Komarnicki. Want me to spell it?"

I sprang up walking toward him with an attitude, because he didn't exactly look like a King of the Hill prospect to me. He held his ground, though, so I raised my voice even louder. "You got my bike, and I want to know where you got it!"

I grabbed the handlebars, then turned the bike upside down, pointing to the underside of the crossbar. "You see that 'K'? It's the Komarnicki brand."

He coughed, looking at the ground like he was trying to figure out what to do next. The marble crowd had vanished, so he had no recourse of ganging me. It was

75

him and me, and he was standing on shifty acorns.

"What's your name?" I asked him again.

"Ralphie," he said.

"Where'd you get my bike?"

"A kid down the street sold it to me for ten bucks," he brayed.

"Look, Ralphie," I said. "Walk me home, I'll show you where I live, and you bring that kid around to my house and I'll settle the score with him. And you better get your ten bucks back. Where do you live anyway?"

"Over on Third, near Crosby," he answered reluctantly.

"Ah! That's right down from the Boys' Detention Home and Reform School," I said. "I know Mrs. Gladwyne, the lady who runs the place, so just bring your buddy around to my house and I'll introduce him to her."

As we walked my bike down the alley to my house, this kid really looked dejected. I sensed he felt exactly the way I'd been feeling since Saturday morning. He didn't wave when he slinked away, his hands buried deep in his pockets. I waited till he turned at Crosby Street, and as I wheeled my bike down my narrow alley, a funny thought came to me: "He's walking by Walt Seigle's house right about now."

Not a reportable thing happened all week. At least not until Saturday morning, when I settled into my fourth-row seat at the Washington Theatre to watch Ken Maynard rid the town of a gang of deadbeats. And guess what! There was Ralphie in the seat right in front of me.

Just as the cattle rustlers started a stampede through the canyon, I leaned forward with a mouthful of Jujy Fruits and whispered loudly, "Hey, Ralphie, did you ever get your ten bucks back?"

76

He turned, adjusted his eyes in the dark, then said, "Yeah! Yeah! I got my money back. I told my neighbor you knew Mrs. Gladwyne who ran the reform school down the street, and he whipped out the ten right on the spot."

I handed Ralphie a couple of Jujy Fruits and leaned back to enjoy the show.

When the show ended on the usual high note of rights wronged and justice done, I ran home, lifted the two lead soldiers from my cigar box, and hustled down to Kresge's Five and Dime. I entered, saddled up to the soldier display, waited till the counter lady wasn't looking, slid the soldiers out of my pocket, and placed them in perfect formation with the others.

When the counter lady turned my way, I handed her a quarter and said with a smile, "This is in payment for a molding kit to make my own soldiers."

"You returned just as you promised." she said.

"Yes, ma'am, I almost always do," I said.

I left the store at peace with the world, glad that I didn't know who stole my bike, gladder still to get it back.

And just as I walked beneath the Pennsy Railroad underpass, I spotted Officer Kandravi, my arch-nemesis, puffing his way along Edgmont Avenue. As he passed, giving me his usual glare, I smiled as I thought, "Every kid oughta be able to get away with something, especially if he gets the chance to make it right."

The Oxblood Incident

A vise-like shoulder grip cancelled all options to exit as an apron-clad grim reaper hustled me past the frozen foods to the A & P's back room, then hoisted me atop stacked cartons of Campbell's soup cans. A bass baritone command erupted: "Empty your pockets, kid!"

I complied slowly, one pocket at a time.

"What's the bulge behind the right knee, kid?"

"What bulge?"

"Come clean, kid, or I'll X-ray you!"

I slid my hand through the torn pocket in my knickers clear down to my leg band, slowly retrieving an economy-sized can of oxblood shoe polish.

"Got a receipt, kid?"

Avoiding his eyes (and his question), I stared at the gum-pocked cement floor.

"What's your name, kid? Where do you live? How old are you? Ever been to reform school?"

I responded with mumbled truth to each question he fired at me.

Mr. Bass Baritone walked to the wall phone, dialed, conversed in muffled tones, hung up, and tossed his apron at a nearby chair. "Might as well relax, kid. You'll be here a while."

"Watch him," he admonished his assistant, who was parked by the room's only exit. "He's wearing Joe Lapchick sneakers."

As Mr. Bass Baritone left the room, I sat, head bowed, pondering my fate. My mental boxcars were rumbling down dual faulty tracks:

- The shame of defaming the family name fanned into the imagined pain inflicted by Pop's strap in just retribution.

- The cost of a life of crime—stained at the age of 12 by a can of oxblood!

They'd caught me, squeezed me through a Maytag wringer of fear, and flattened me. They'd confiscated my "borrowed" oxblood, limited my livelihood, and now they had a fix on all my traceable statistics. The burden of guilt vied with the burden of a blemished future as I sat atop the stack of cartons with the Campbell's Soup Kid smiling up at me.

* * *

It had all started that morning when school let out early. Something about a war bond drive. Kay Kyser and his band, complete with Ish Kabibble and vocalist Ginny Simms, were honoring Chester with a visit, appearing at the Stanley Theatre to entertain the locals and hopefully stir up a fervor to invest in the war effort.

But I had other plans for the morning. We already had three stars hanging in our front window (for brothers Mickey and Joe and our brother-in-law Rich), and I figured that was all the investment I needed to make. With no coins in my pocket and very few in my Christmas

Club account, I opted to use this unexpected school holiday to shine my way into some needed cash.

Grabbing my shoeshine box, I traversed the back-alley route to town and set up my business at Sixth and Edgmont. As I squatted atop my seat-cushioned box, scanning the passing parade for scuffed shoes, I reflected on the portable wonder on which I sat. The carved pedestal of a foot was fashioned from one of brother John's Florsheims. The wood grain buried under seven layers of shellac I'd applied in Mr. Ridenour's woodshop at Smedley Junior High was smooth to the touch. All corners were rounded with a file, all nails evenly spaced. The inset carrying handle, the width of a roll of quarters, was fashioned for quick grabs and speedy retreats necessitated by sudden appearances of local cops who frowned upon street urchin activities.

My reverie was interrupted by the approach of a dandy decked out in a three-piece suit and a picture-

perfect Stetson. crossing Sixth Street with the confidence of a ward boss. He carried a folded *Racing Form,* no doubt acquired at Roder's Newsstand a block away. Leaning against the cut-stone wall, he lit a Panatela cigar, placed his right foot on the pedestal of my box, and said, "Oxblood, kid, and watch the socks!"

I rummaged through my double-compartment shoeshine box, lifting out the felt rags and some Liquid White in a brush-top bottle, then each can of polish one by one—tan, brown, black, cordovan, even a creamy blue I'd lifted from Vicky's closet. But no oxblood.

Anyway, a new lesson was added to my growing tapeworm of street smarts when the gent took his foot off my shoeshine box, looked down into my entrepreneurial eyes, and replied, "No oxblood, no shine."

He walked briskly around the corner, disappearing up the granite steps of the Pennsy station to catch the Chester/Wilmington/ Baltimore/Washington Express. I'd had my shine money and my tip spent already, and I'd never even heard the tinkle of the coins. Mom had been right when she'd offered the pithy wisdom, "Never count your chickens before they're hatched."

I was so mad I spit out my entire five-stick wad of gum, still sweet with spearmint juice. I just sat there on my box as the train pulled away, spewing soot with a vengeance as it gathered momentum toward Wilmington.

"Now what, dummy?" I mused. "Without inventory to match the need, you're dead!"

A shrill whistle halted my reverie, and I looked up to see Officer Kandravi advancing on me. I leapt up, grabbed my box, ran down Sixth, and cut through the alley behind Edgmont Avenue. I took a brief look at the Wilson footballs in Briggs Sporting Goods, turned the corner, and was met with the nostril-quivering aroma coming from Jimmy's Texas Wieners. The pungent fragrance was pumped out of the 8' x 12' eatery by a giant, greasy fan planted in its window to pull in the passing stream of pedestrians. But I didn't have enough money to indulge my inclination, so I walked east on Seventh and entered through the back door of our three-storied, bay-windowed house. No one was home.

It was a rare feeling to be home alone. I poured a glass of milk and added a double shot of Ovaltine. As I downed my drink, a plan of action was hatched. I left the way I came, hiding my shoeshine box in the backyard shed, then sprinted the three blocks to the Great Atlantic and Pacific Tea Company, which everybody had affectionately shortened to the A & P.

I entered and strolled the aisles, trying to assume the appearance of a kid sent to the store by his mother. I checked out the lay of the store, paused at the shoe polish section, spotted the Kiwi oxblood can, applied a sleight of hand to drop the "borrowed" contribution into the right leg of my pocketless knickers, and nonchalantly sauntered toward the exit. I paused at the door, this time assuming the casual posture of a bored kid waiting for his sister.

Suddenly I felt the gentle but firm, vise-like grip on my shoulder. My turning head caught a glimpse of four eyes and two apron-clad men whom I'd previously seen at the vegetable table watering the lettuce.

* * *

So there I sat, waiting for my execution. Mr. Bass Baritone reentered the room, walked over, looked me square in the eyes, and with grim countenance and measured words said, "Your parents will hear about this! Now get outta here!"

Swallowing hard I sprang from my perch, sauntered in controlled haste to the entrance, pushed freedom's door open, then backtracked the way I came. I passed Sixth and Edgmont and Sun Ray Drug. At Smith's Newsstand, I cut down the oblique alley at Sixth leading to Welsh, shot past the Colonial Hotel, Greco's Bakery, Massi's Parking Lot, Charlie Peck's store, Patrycia's Barber Shop, and Joe Miller's bar, and finally darted down my own narrow side alley. Entering the back door, I walked through the kitchen, climbed the serpentine steps up to my room, lay face up on my squeaky bed, and squirmed as if I'd swallowed a can of earthworms. How would I explain this infamy to Mom and Pop, to sister Mary and sister Vicky, to John, Dan, George, Paul, and Jim ... and the brothers fighting the war in progress?

How does a kid explain away shame inflicted on a name my parents wore like a medal of honor, a name now splattered with oxblood polish? Pop labored six days a week, 10 hours a day at Roser's Restaurant on Welsh Street. Mom worked 19 hours a day at home, seven days a week. And me??? Their sixth son had slid like an electric eel through the corridors of informal and formalized learning until this frozen moment of shame. My mental pain peaked at migraine levels. I felt the pangs of self-pity rise to a flood level. Suddenly I realized what I must do.

I MUST RUN AWAY FROM HOME—before the cops come to the door, handcuff me, and haul me away, before Pop comes home from work and lays a much-needed strap on my "zadook." This was a word I heard only when Pop swung into tough love, along with the words I knew only phonetically, "Ya te be dom per strachke." They were always spoken in a low, modulated, syncopated tone as the pupils in Pop's eyes enlarged and the leather strap was unbuckled.

"They'll miss me when I'm gone," mused my puffed-up pride. "They'll beg me to come back home."

The shame on the family name, the fear of multiple welts from the well-aimed strap converged on me as I bit into my pillow. If I was going to go, I'd better do it now while Mom was shopping. She must have taken Jim and Paul with her. George no doubt was at the Boyd Diner peeling spuds. Dan was probably setting pins at the Ches/Penn Bowling Alley.

I scrounged around for as many coins as I could find in the White Owl cigar box I kept in the closet. I fingered through the incomplete set of Sino-Japanese War cards, trying to assess what I should take with me. I tossed two rumpled T-shirts, four unmatched socks, and a diamond-patterned sweater (no sleeves) into a pillowcase and headed for the back stairs to the kitchen.

I impulsively stopped to open the Cold Spot icebox, a giant hunger station backed against the middle section of

84

the bay window in full view of the alley. I threw open the door, stepped back, and beheld the greatest array of assorted foods ever packed into so limited a space: half a ham hock with a protruding bone (Mom will make great soup out of that baby); two giant-sized cans of melba peaches from Quality Market; assorted cheeses; two quarts of Supplee-Wills-Jones milk (one chocolate, one whole milk); a box of Tastykakes (three to a pack); a bottle of Frank's Black Cherry Wishniak (no cap and just itching to be swigged down to four ounces, which I promptly did); two huge tomatoes; three heads of leafy lettuce; two family-sized jars of Smuckers' Jelly (grape and peach); and a half-eaten pear with withered brown skin.

I cut short the admiration of the Cold Spot's contents and closed the door with a sense of overpowering loss. My stomach churned, but not from hunger. Turning to exit through the kitchen, I noticed the marble I'd stuffed in a little hole in the linoleum floor between the two rooms— a marble to thwart the out-crawling of black widow spiders from their webs below. Was it Joe who had warned me not to descend into the dungeon, the clay-dirt cellar that reeked with cat droppings? Was it he who told me that if a black widow bit me I'd swell up like a balloon bigger than Officer Kandravi's stomach? That I'd lose all my hair like Mr. Huber, who nightly occupied the end seat at the Boyd Diner counter, wolfing down blue plate specials?

My thoughts ran like dysentery as I walked through the kitchen, then the attached shed where the rollers on Mom's Maytag held a blue shirt in their grip. It reminded me of the blue tongue of the German police dog that always tried to run George and me down in Deshong Park whenever we ransacked the seckel pear trees.

No time for visuals, though, or associations or nostalgia or any form of backward-glancing sentiment. I was a fugitive. I was on the lam. In flight. I'd write Mom and Pop a postcard from some strange city. I'd seen the names of cities galore pasted on the sides of boxcars as freight trains clacked through Chester, heading north, heading south. They often slowed down while passing through town, some of them rolling through slower than I could walk, hobos peering out of the half-opened sliding doors, wearing heavy coats even in summer to cushion the effect of the hard, splintery floors.

I unlocked the back gate, then walked to the mouth of the alley. I paused there, looking left, then right, and beheld a sight etched forever more on my mind. As I looked around the corner of the house, I saw the most treasured object of affection ever assembled into a human body. It was Mom, trudging home from Collins Grocery Store. She squinted into the direct sunlight, walking slowly past Carmen's Hoagie Shop and pausing slightly as she passed Tucker's Pool Hall. As she crossed the street to home, I framed her face with John's Small Profit Store in the background.

I was still in the alleyway, flat up against our house with my pillowcase duffel bag between my legs, as I watched her step slowly off the granite curbstone, looking carefully both ways. She was wearing a babushka knotted under her chin, and her dress was below mid-calf and patterned in soft pastels. I remembered going with her when she bought her black leather Enna Jettick shoes, perforated with tiny fashionable holes on the toes. Her hair, her beautiful brown hair, was pulled tightly into a giant bun. I often watched as she stroked it with a fine-tooth comb then suddenly swirled it mysteriously into a tucked twist and impaled it with a long stickpin. She was carrying her puffy shopping bag with its oilcloth texture. It was her favorite for serious shopping, and there were lumps the size of grapefruits on both sides. Celery stalks were peering over the top. It was a movable feast for all at table tonight, and I was running away.

I chanced a peak as Mom labored up the three worn granite steps to the front door. She paused carefully, placing the bag by her knee as she forced the door open. I always had to lift the door slightly by the knob to unjam it and keep it from squeaking when I came in after curfew. I timed Mom's walk down the 10-foot hallway, her right turn into the living room, then another 10 feet into the linoleum-decked refrigerator room. Then, like a paratrooper in free fall, I leapt out of the alley to follow through on my plan to run away.

I waved to Joe, the doughnut-store owner, as I breezed by and to Nick Moretti leaning on the recently installed Duncan parking meter in front of his pop's tailor shop. My dream of one day parading through downtown Chester in a Moretti-made suit dropped out of sight. In fact, my nightmare now was that I would be fitted for a gray suit with a number on the back and forever roam the grounds of Glen Mills Detention Home with visitors restricted to Saturday afternoons.

My mental marquee was as active as the blinking neon sign above the entrance to the 520 Club on Edgmont Avenue:

The Komarnicki Conscience

Upon intense questioning by the Chester Police a local kid confessed to multiple unsolved crimes.

Dave Komarnicki, son of Joseph and Anna of 151 E. Seventh St., Chester, confessed to multiple pilfers today. The list is too long to enumerate or elucidate, but a few notables were:

- The borrowing, on a regular basis, of YMCA towels.

- The stealing of papers, cardboard, scrap iron, and copper from Smedley's Junk Shop—all items he had sold to Mr. Smedley a week before. It is said that he cleverly rearranged the paper,

87

wetting down the middle of the tightly wound bundles, thus adding weight to the booty, for which he was then paid.

- The swiping of a football by him and Barney Massi from Silver's Five & Dime. Dave stated that his intentions had been good but Barney had told him to throw a pass from the sports counter to the entrance door, which he did, but Barney had then fled the store, making him an accomplice. The football was recovered from the Komarnicki shed.

The police also located a dozen pocketknives "borrowed" from Miss Ward's chalk box at Larkin School.

The list was longer than the line outside the State Theatre the day *The Road to Morocco* with Bob Hope and Bing Crosby came to town. I stood mute, transfixed, wrapped in guilt. As I stood on the corner of Sixth and Welsh, in front of Gus Kaffes' father's restaurant, a quick glance up the railroad embankment caught the Philadelphia local just leaving the station. My eye lingered on the visage of a man leaning on the railing of the Pennsylvania Railroad platform above.

It was the railroad dick, his identity announced by his herringbone overcoat and Dick Tracy Stetson. Last winter I'd thrown an icy snowball at the crowd awaiting the Wilmington local, and my Bob ("Rapid Robert") Feller accuracy had caught the railroad dick square in the head, dethroning his hat and arousing his ire. I'd taken shelter behind the outdoor billboard while he'd collected his Stetson and descended the 16 wooden steps to Welsh Street in furious search of the "detention school candidate."

He hadn't caught me then, but the sight of him now was enough to temporarily derail my game plan to ascend the platform steps and hop a slow-moving freight train out of town.

Just then, as fate would have it, I instinctively looked to my left before de-curbing to cross the street and walk Market Street to the river. Despite the fear-inflamed state of my fugitive mind, I caught sight of the *Philadelphia Inquirer* truck turning onto Sixth at Upland, the Wetherill factory looming as a backdrop. The driver raced his trackless train down Sixth, hardly pausing at Madison Street, ignoring Crosby, and pulling to a ritual stop 20 feet from me. The tailgate dropped, and bailed bundles of Saturday early edition *Inquirers* were tossed onto the street. Bobby Berman cut the cross-wires on the bundles, then thrust the papers into the hands of shouting local urchins, who fled in pursuit of sales.

My paperboy instincts overcame my runaway urgings, and I ran across the street, tossing my pillow-cased escape duds behind the outdoor billboard rising against the wall of Pennsy Station. I took as many papers as I could carry and lit out for Third Street (my Broadway). I ducked into the Chester Arms Hotel and sold three. I sold two in Joe Keenan's bar before he spotted me and ordered me out, then ran to Minnetti's, where "magic" descended in the form of the body and face of a barmaid who ever after thawed chilly memories like a hot water bottle on January cold feet.

I'd scanned her jet-black hair and her face many times before as she stood before the bar, a magnet to all patrons sober enough to observe—sleek, inviting, an intoxicating welder's flash relief to any ship fitter stopping by. This moment was a baptismal for me. As the barmaid fixed me in the laser beam of her beautiful black eyes, she waved me toward her, leaned forward, and gave me a maternal hug reserved for war heroes, one that introduced me to manly feelings not yet understood as a kid. She then ordered an Errol Flynn type to buy all my newspapers. He promptly unpocketed a horse-choker of a bankroll, peeling off and palming me with a Jackson note—more cash than I'd pocket in a month of shines.

Those warm, beguiling barmaid eyes and the abrupt change in my fortunes snapped the cords of my fear of consequences. I left Minnetti's intoxicated, pausing at the door and grinning back into the smoke-filled room. I spread my arms heavenward, as if to fly away like Superman. I blew a kiss toward my benefactor, then with a salute of gratitude shouted "God bless America!" as I pocketed my $20 bill and threw open the door in nimble exit. Running like a greyhound to Sixth and Welsh, where I settled up with Bobby Berman for the papers, I retrieved my pillowcase runaway satchel from behind the billboard and headed toward home in full Mummer's Strut, stopping only long enough to buy a couple of chili dogs, topped with mustard and sauerkraut, at Jimmy's.

Negative thoughts of family shame diminished along with the wieners. Burping my way home, I paused to pick up a pint of hand-packed peach ice cream at Charlie Peck's store—a love offering for Mom from her number-eight child, just in case some appeasement was necessary.

I was ready for the worst. But the worst never came. The police never knocked. The A &P duo who caught me in the act never went public.

I returned to the scene of the crime the next day, bought two cans of oxblood, a head of lettuce, and a diamond-studded Duncan yo-yo. The backroom twosome watched as I sauntered to the cashier and counted out the cost in quarters. I paused at the entrance, shot a backward glance over my shoulder, and caught a wink and a smile from Mr. Bass Baritone. I returned the gesture as I pushed open the swinging door. Once outside, it occurred to me that he and his buddy had been kids once. Maybe they carried a reprieve for their own oxblood incident and decided to pass it on.

I walked to the curb, leaned against the parking meter, sucked in the crisp September air reminiscent of a Vicks menthol inhaler, and peppered it out in staccato ripples like a trumpeter triple-tonguing a high note. Just then a red truck lumbered by, door open on the driver's side, and the mustached, bespectacled man at the wheel turned his head to look me full in the face. I quickly identified him as Chester's part-time truant officer, whose frequent visits to our home gave his face top billing on the list of the Most Feared Faces in Town.

His knowing look whispered, "One of these days you're off to Glen Mills, kid, for your repeated dancing on the edge ...." I stuck my tongue out as he belched his exhaust toward the post office.

I turned to walk Edgmont toward the Sixth Street railroad underpass and in the process slipped my newly acquired yo-yo onto the second knuckle of my right hand.

I yo-yo'd my crooked path up Market, even stepping into the street to gain the space needed to execute "Sleeping Beauty," and almost lost my composure and my life as I stepped off the curb approaching Woolworth's Five & Dime. I was in the midst of inventing a new trick when June Rowe stepped out of the store, spotted me, smiled, and kept walking toward Seventh. She was Ingrid Bergman, Hedy Lamarr, and Jeanne Crain combined. To garner her smile and watch her move down the street was like swallowing a bottle of niacin tablets. I followed her like a hound dog past Birney's Cigars and Weinberg's Department Store, then lost her in the milling crowd as she crossed Seventh, passed Adam's Clothing Store, and headed toward the Boyd Theater.

Just then my reverie and dream-walking were blown away by the trumpet-lipped orchestrator of traffic, none other than Officer Kandravi, who kept the flow in motion in the main aorta of town. With mixed emotions, I leaned against the steel pole at Speare Brothers to watch this 5' 4" king of the road handle the ebb and flow through the three-street convergence of Seventh, Welsh, and Edgmont. To me, Kandravi was a nail in my bicycle tires, an aborter of shoeshines. I needed the eyes of a horsefly to watch for his evasive approach. He was the preeminent actor in his own domain, always on the watch for anyone horsing around on his stage.

Suddenly a jolt of power and acumen surged through me. It seemed to rise from my tingling toes rocking in the sublime comfort of Joe Lapchick Converse sneakers. It warmed my massive calf muscles, tightly pressed by the stretch band of my knickers. It spread through my loins, caught fire in my chest, and came to life as I re-indexed my Duncan and launched into my routine. First, a "Walk the Doggie" that stayed down the entire 30 feet of Speare's glitter-sprinkled, satin-smooth pavement, then a flat-out flawless "Sleeping Beauty." Window-shoppers craned their necks to watch me, as the crowd shifted up the sidewalk. Next came an "Around the World," a "Three-Leaf Clover," an "Eat the Spaghetti," a "Rock the Cradle," a "Shooting Star," and an "Into the Pocket."

With each textbook execution, the critical mass of onlookers grew. Oohs and aahs followed, clapping trickled through, and the knot of people spilled onto Seventh Street like an out-of-control glazed doughnut in the making. Tightening the trick string with another "Sleeping Beauty," I announced my finale as an attempt to break the authentic Guinness World Record in "Loop the Loops." I challenged the crowd to count along as I launched into my eye-hand coordination.

There are moments in life that define us, that live ever after as existential moments, frozen in slow motion frames, tucked into the silent connective linkages of the brain—moments that, if mastered, lead on to a true greatness. I sensed this to be such a moment as the count began. When it reached 10, self-consciousness faded. When the growing chant reached 25, my concentration on timing melted into awareness of individual faces in the growing mass of onlookers.

- I saw Luke Howard counting. Double-breasted, pot-bellied Sol Weinberg was counting. Bobby Berman, masticating an unlit cigar, was counting. Eddie Morrell was just smiling.

- Danny Murtaugh stood next to Mickey Vernon, both of them wide-eyed with controlled approval.

- Danny Yokis was pumping his chest with pride.

- Bill Cleuce stood next to Dr. Schultz, both looking a little piqued at being stopped by a crowd while in route to their handball game at the YMCA.

- At the count of 102, Mr. Moskowitz asked Emil Huber if the kid with the yo-yo was a Komarnicki.

- Shorty D'Iignazio's face was glued to the seamless, silent strokes of my trick string.

- Matt Zabitka started scribbling notes when I hit 150.

- Like a giant amoeba, the crowd reconfigured but kept the count alive.

- At 206, Mr. Briggs of sports store notoriety appeared.

- Then came Jospeh M. Joseph, vice principal of Smedley and my Optimist Club sponsor— bespectacled, bald as an eagle, grinning with the pride of an adoptive father.

- Sweeney, Hopkins, and Clyde turned in tandem toward me as they paused to cross Seventh and

93

Edgmont, no doubt breaking for lunch at the State House.

- At about 327, George Boyd of diner fame sauntered down Seventh and had to walk in the street. He looked as though he were heading toward our house a block away to commandeer brother George to peel potatoes.

Testing the limits of even the most ardent admirers is rarely possible, but the shifting, multi-faced core remained to the end, and the end came abruptly. My sizzling string, tensiled to the last twist, suddenly snapped and my diamond-studded Duncan took flight over the head of Miss Ward, my beloved first grade teacher, and met its resistance at the base of Kandravi's officially capped skull at Seventh and Welsh. Kandravi turned, blew his whistle with a window-shattering shrill, and with yo-yo in hand lurched toward me.

If it weren't for the admiring crowd, I'd be history. Kandravi eyeballed me, did a 360-degree take on the mass of admirers now clapping with the fanned force of a team of Clydesdales. He placed my yo-yo into the palm of my hand and with a razor strop voice said, "Move out, kid, you're blocking traffic."

As I crossed Seventh and Welsh in route home, the venerable hand of none other than John McClure patted my shoulder. My head felt lighter than a feather as he proposed, "See me when you're eighteen, kid. I've got a job waiting for your talent."

I levitated to a hover as I floated by Caruso Music Store, a saxophone's sweet sounds playing, *"I'll never smile again until I smile at you."* I floated past Charlie Peck's Ice Cream Emporium and came to rest on the smooth, penny-pitching sidewalk of home: 151 E. Seventh.

Pop's words of biblical wisdom whispered in my soul,

"It is more blessed to give than to receive." I was tempted to query him on my puzzlement as to how a kid could have it both ways.

The guys at the A & P had given me a break by not squealing, and to boot I'd received an $18 tip and the Wall of Fame applause of an admiring town. With the gratitude of someone snatched from the jaws of perdition, I paused a moment before pushing the front door open. I'd figure out the answer to Pop's proverb later. Right now, it was soup and sandwich time and then basketball at the Y.

13 Is a Lucky Number

Bobby Berman stooped to clip the three wired bundles of *Philadelphia Inquirers* (Late-Night War Edition) that he'd stacked by my feet. "No returns, Davey," he bellowed in his gravel voice, cigar stub clenched in the left corner of his mouth. "Hustle till you sell out, and this route is yours!" He eyed me through thick rimless glasses, then turned, took three steps to his Hudson, hopped in, and sped away down Lloyd Street toward Chestertown.

"Boy! This is a choice nightly route," I thought to myself, as I sized up my high-visibility location right beside the guard station at the huge Ford Assembly Plant. "If I sell out tonight, I'll be a captain in Bobby Berman's army of hustlers. And it couldn't come along at a better time—my 13th birthday!"

With hands tucked into the pouch of my hooded cotton jacket, I stood behind the pile of papers waiting for.... I wasn't sure what I was waiting for. I only knew I had to hawk that whole stack—250 papers—so I could settle with Bobby Berman by the ten o'clock curfew or I'd lose the route on my first night.

The guard standing in the doorway of his station seemed to sense my edginess. "Relax, kid," he said, "but watch your papers, keep a hand on the pile, then fork over a paper when you get the money."

"Thanks for the advice, sir," I said. The guard—a tall, slim, bespectacled man—looked familiar to me. "Sir, do you live in Sun Village? Did I see you in Johnson's Hardware Store last Saturday morning?"

"Yeah, kid, I live on Remington Street. Gotta son your age, goes to Smedley. His name's Aloysius—Aloysius McGrann."

"Hey, Al's a buddy of mine," I told him. I was about to blurt out that Al and I had recently hookied school to go swimming at the Leiper Quarry, but luckily the eight o'clock whistle ended our dialogue.

Workers moved out of the Ford plant like a swarm of locusts. Those hungry for the latest war news rushed over, and in no time the pile had shrunk from belly-high to below my knees. I held out my left hand for the money and returned change if the men lingered for it. They were orderly, grabbing what they paid for and then moving away in silence to focus on the headlines.

I stood at my post, watching the crowd of men. Some were sitting on wooden benches, straining to read under dim lights. Others were eating sandwiches they pulled out of battered lunch pails, leaning against the barbed-wire fence and shifting bites from cheek to cheek like giant squirrels. Others just milled around, stretching, rubbing weary eyes, and jaw-boning with their buddies. I drank it all in while sifting the nickels, dimes, quarters, and half-dollars that were filling my jacket pouch.

98

"Man, these coins feel good," I mused. "Pop told me once that the love of money is the root of evil, but it isn't money that I love. I love the look in Mom's eyes when I hand her a fistful of coins at night, and I love caramels, Bolsters, Milky Way candy bars, Dixie Cups, Tastykakes, gumdrops, Butterfingers, and sodas sipped slowly so they last longer. I love kites, model airplanes, yo-yos, cap guns, chocolate sundaes, milkshakes, jawbreakers, popsicles, Jujy Fruits, Saturday double features at the Washington Theater, and trips to Riverview Beach on the Wilson Line. I love all the stuff Mom has no extra money to give me."

A shrill whistle pierced the cloudy night sky, calling workers back to bury the enemy with production.

Thanking Mr. McGrann for helping me on my first night on the job, I tucked the unsold papers behind the shoulder strap Bobby Berman had given me to hold them to my rib cage, then started heading up Lloyd Street towards Third to begin my 15-block search for sales in every club, restaurant, and bar. Mr. Berman's words goaded me on: "Sell out, Davey! No returns!"

The newspaper was thicker tonight, but I didn't mind the load. My back could take it, and my jacket could weather the rain if it came. A few weeks ago, I'd practiced pulling a paper out of my stack, creasing it, then handing it over with upturned palm.

"Every paper I sell, I'll look 'em in the eye, smile, and rip off a 'thanks.'" I reminded myself. "Quick action with a smile gets many a nickel for a three-cent paper. Tonight's no sentimental journey; it's survival measured in nickels and dimes. I gotta hustle, gotta use whatever flair I can muster."

I had a lot of time to think while trudging along.

"What if I get waylaid in one of these alleys? I'm alone in unknown territory, the street lamps are dim, and

99

a crouching dog could leap out when I'm least expecting it. Will I sell out before it rains? I feel moisture on my forehead right now. I'm okay, but what about my papers? Wet papers don't sell. And what about the curfew? What if I don't sell out? Will Mr. Berman take this route away from me?"

At Larkin School, Miss Ginter once read to us about how George Washington had walked this very road into Chester after losing the Battle of Brandywine and how he'd later written the whole sad story in his journal while sitting in a tavern on Market Street.

I paused after crossing Second Street, which had been called Post Road during Colonial times. In my mind's eye, General Washington suddenly appeared, leading his ragged troops into Chester. Some were carried on makeshift stretchers, while others limped along with a leg wrapped with a burlap bandage, leaning on the shoulder of a fellow soldier. The general himself was on foot, too, perhaps to rest his weary horse or maybe to identify with the suffering of his retreating troops. His posture was as erect as a ramrod, his demeanor resolute.

Then, snapped from my trance, I glanced at the headline of the *Philadelphia Inquirer* in my hand: "Germans Retreating from Salerno Plain." My meandering thoughts shifted to my brother Mickey, walking a muddy road in Burma in an endless line of war-weary soldiers. Was Mickey limping? Was he leaning on a friend? Was he wounded?

Then, peering into the fog sweeping in from the Delaware River, I whispered. "Thanks, General Washington. Thanks for leaving us an example of keeping the faith."

I then turned to face my own journey, my battle to keep the faith and win the right to sell papers at the Ford Assembly Plant every night, to earn money to keep the home fires burning—coal for the furnace, clothes on our backs for the coming winter.

"If I don't win my battle tonight, *I'll* be history," I reminded myself. "I'll be forced to return to the nightly hustle through the streets of downtown Chester, where competition is fierce and tempers edgy, running to reach the taprooms first. Tonight I gotta sell every written word strapped to my body."

Reaching Third Street, checking traffic both ways, I cut diagonally across Lloyd Street to Tony Marino's Tavern. I breathed deep, unlatched the heavy double doors, crossed the threshold, and—bingo!—immediate endorsement. The bartender waved me forward to the open side of the bar, pinched a paper from the middle of my stack, and dropped a dime into my palm.

"*Che si dice?*" he said.

"*Benie, grazie,*" I responded, dipping into my limited stockpile of Italian vocabulary.

When the belly-to-the-bar lineup of Sons of Italy heard me call out in their lingo, hands shot into pockets faster than Roy Rogers could hoist his holstered gun. Five papers were tweaked from my stack, and five nickels joined the jingle in my pocket. I gave them a flamboyant, Caruso-in-concert smile as I bowed my way out the door.

Once outside I shouted "Huzzah!," a word of exclamation I'd heard my buddy Poe Parramore shout out after he'd sunk a half-court set-shot to win a basketball game at the YMCA. Next door to Tony Marino's was a billiard room. I had a budding interest in the game but resisted the urge to enter and pick up some pointers on its art and science.

I decided instead to work the room at Iacono's Restaurant next door. I dashed in, sold two, pocketed the change, and then contentedly continued west, pausing to check the window display of Puragino's Cigar Store. Nostril-phobia caused an involuntary nose-twitch at the aroma, but, man, what an inventory! The window display featured every cigar this side of Cuba—White Owls, Philly-Blunts, Panatelas, Garcia y Vegas, Webster's, Cincos, Robert Burns, Muriel's.

Suddenly a whisper with Pop's Slavic accent rang in the inner ear of my conscience: "Chewing tobacco rots the gums, and cigar smoke causes Blue Lung."

How Pop knew about Blue Lung, I'd never know. Brother George and I occasionally smoked cattails, which we handpicked from the swamps in Essington. We'd light them, wrap them in notebook paper, then take puffs. Come to think about it, I did see George's face turn blue, but his gum line still looked okay.

Continuing west, I paused again on the sidewalk outside DiCostanza's. History books credit Columbus with discovering America, and DiCostanza claims credit for the creation of the first hoagie, a sandwich that hooks you for life once you've tasted it. I walked in, but the crowd wasn't buying papers. They were peering over the glass protector that shielded the unsliced meat from coughs and sneezes.

I stood off to the side, watching as customers barked out preferences: "Hey, Augusto, more oregano, more provolone, hot peppers, onions, oil, prosciutto, and whatever else you gotta." The back shelves featured items these immigrants had been tasting since childhood.

I stepped outside, stomach growling for a taste of what I'd left behind. I poked along until distracted by a tailor working late in Peter Coelho's shop. He was stitching a sleeve onto a navy-blue, pinstriped suit coat mounted on a torso-shaped mannequin. His bald head gleamed under a focused ceiling light, a tape measure hung around his shirt collar. He was a surgeon suturing cloth—intense, focused, a true craftsman.

"Brother John has a pinstriped suit," I thought to myself. "It's hanging in his closet, draped on a wooden hanger pinching the pants tight across the wooden strip. It'll hang there until he returns from the war. Maybe I'll inherit that suit someday, but I'd rather see John wearing it, turning heads as he walks up Market Street on a Friday night."

This pleasant reverie engaged me until I looked into Pompilli's Barber Shop window, where a generously endowed patron reclined with lathered face in the front chair. Pompilli, straight razor in hand, was poised to orchestrate his tonsorial skill while slicing gingerly around the patron's prominent Roman nose.

Reaching Broomall Street, I decided to backtrack towards town. Before crossing, I paused for a truck to pass and watched as it pulled up to a loading dock labeled "NIGHT OWL CURB SERVICE." I crossed, then mounted the curb at Saint Luke's Episcopal Church and stood gaping at its blood-red arched doors. The stone sanctuary seemed strong and ageless, exuding a feeling of permanence. I started to voice a prayer as a man walked by, checking me out with peripheral vision. I waited until he passed me, then whispered, "May those who worship here find peace only God can bring."

It was while walking away that I remembered asking my friend Danny Bartkow, "Why the red doors on all Episcopal churches?"

He'd told me that the red symbolizes the blood shed by Jesus Christ when crucified on the cross and that Christians believe it was the blood of Jesus Christ that paid the penalty for the sins of the world. I could still see the look on Danny's face and hear the sincerity in his voice as he told me this. I didn't completely understand his answer, but it did help me understand the lyrics to a hymn Pop often sang while sitting in his armchair in our living room:

Would you be free from the burden of sin?
There's power in the blood, power in the blood;
Would you o'er evil a victory win?
There's wonderful power in the blood.

There is power, power,
Wonder-working power
In the blood of the Lamb;
There is power, power,
Wonder-working power
In the precious blood of the Lamb.

The flickering neon light steered me, like a moth, to Colletta's Tavern, just east of Lomokin Street. I barged in, made a quick sale, then a quick departure. Ah! Next door sat DiMeglio's Pool Hall, and this time a sudden uncontrollable urge vacuumed me inside, where I frittered away precious selling time watching a kid a couple of years my senior clear the table of 14 balls. His silk-smooth stroke, his moves around the pool table in a semi-hypnotic focus, mesmerized me. I made no sales, but the observations that I tucked away I'd practice tomorrow at the YMCA.

"Imagine a kid running a whole rack of balls," I thought as I left. "Maybe someday I'll do that."

As I shuffled towards Pennell Street, a muffled growl stopped me in my tracks. I turned instinctively, then stepped back as a muzzled German police dog leapt from a narrow side-alley, slamming its jaw against the protective shield of newspapers strapped across my chest. Gulping hard, I swallowed my wad of gum, but I stood my ground, staring it down as it turned to circle me. Its owner called it from an elevated porch, where he sat in a rocking chair, and the dog slinked away in whining obedience.

Cupping his hands, Mr. No-Leash hollered, "Rex won't bite. He's harmless!"

Looking towards the porch, I mimicked his outcry with my own cupped hands: "What's the muzzle for if Rex is harmless?"

Waving his hand, he sarcastically answered, "On your way, kid, don't push it!!"

I did go on my way, but I walked curbside, eyeing all alleys, as I headed toward Pennell Street. I calmed my jangled nerves by replacing my swallowed gum with two sticks from my back pocket.

"This is going to be a long night and this Pilgrim's got to make progress," I reminded myself.

Crossing the street, I almost got creamed by a man pedaling a bike—no light on the handlebars, but, okay, it was my fault for slanting across the street between two parked cars. I threw up my hands to apologize as the cyclist looked back, but he raised a clenched fist and blitzed me with a few unmentionables while he pedaled away.

Unfazed by the berating I'd received, I walked into the Lloyd Athletic Club as if they expected me, sold three papers, and then lingered to look at the gallery of framed pictures of sporting events hosted at Lloyd Field over the years. As I gazed at the photos of great moments in football, baseball, rodeo, and boxing history, I suddenly felt like a visiting reporter with a press pass.

"Aha! Pictures of Freddie Sammons and Johnny Fry," I noted.

It brought back memories. I'd stood ringside the night Johnnie Fry KO'd a guy in the first round. The second punch Johnny threw, the guy hit the deck and didn't twitch a muscle. Johnny was a local legend. Just watching him rivet the punching bag as he worked out at the Y gym, shadowboxing, skipping rope, dancing on his toes, was worth the price of a ticket.

"Maybe someday I'll write about all my memories hanging on this wall," I thought.

On the way out, while stopping for a drink at the watercooler in the hallway, I leaned too close to the stream, and the water hit my nose, splashed into my eyes, and landed on my papers.

"What else, you boob?" I scolded myself. "Imagine climbing into the ring with Sammons or Fry when you can't even handle a drink of water!"

I cut my inventory by one at Zachetti's Restaurant next door. My customer, a middle-aged man of girth, wore red suspenders and, as added insurance, a wide brown belt.

"Whew! I'm glad Pop doesn't have one that wide," I mused, remembering the numerous, well-deserved belt-strappings I'd received over the years.

The man stood up to dig deep into his pocket, eventually scooping to the bottom to pull out a nickel. He then waited patiently with upturned palm for his two cents change. During this labor-intense transaction, I checked out his meal: liver and onions.

"Onions are one thing," I contemplated. "I can linger over the smell of fried onions any day and even ask for more on my cheesesteak at Stackey's, but liver? Liver tastes worse than a bite of Fels Naptha soap, which Pop introduced me to, compliments of an expansive, uncensored vocabulary picked up from Yondi Martin."

As I breezed by the American Grocery Store, the gastronomic outlook improved considerably. Spotting a slightly bruised pear in the sidewalk display, I scooped it up and without remorse took a big bite of its succulent flesh. A verse of Scripture, memorized at Third

106

Presbyterian Summer Bible School, flashed into my mind: *"Thou shall not muzzle the ox while it treadeth out the corn."* Here I was, on my 13th birthday, twisting Scripture to justify the pilfering of a wounded pear. I wolfed it down in massive, juice-trickling bites while continuing on toward Pennell Street.

Crossing quickly, I ducked into the restaurant on the corner. There were no sales to be made, but the counterman looked friendly and I hit him with three questions I'd been storing up.

"Could I please have a glass of water?" was my first.

He nodded, and I took a slow, gurgling swallow from the slightly chipped glass of lukewarm water he handed over.

I then asked, "Do you think it will rain tonight?"

With hands tucked in his front pockets, he casually walked to the window, peered out, then up, turned, and said, "Looks like it."

I then brought out the last, most important question: "Do you mind if I use your bathroom?"

"You mean the men's room?" he corrected me.

"Yeah, men's room."

He pointed toward the rear.

"Muchas gracias," I said, pulling out another language from my linguistic inventory. I moved hurriedly in the direction of his pointing finger, urged on by acute kidney pressure. There were no Scott paper towels, so I wiped my hands on my Levi's.

Waving thanks on my way out, I advanced quickly toward Saint George's Hall, hoping to cut some slack on my muscle-strained back, taut from the counterbalance needed to support my load.

"How come Saint George's Hall is here on Third Street in an Italian neighborhood?" I wondered, as I crossed the street to enter.

I walked uncontested through several rooms, selling half a dozen papers to men scattered throughout, some at the bar, some seated in plush leather chairs enjoying the castle-like seclusion only membership can bring. It suddenly hit me that I was yet to set foot in the official territory of Little Italy.

"Saint George is the patron saint of England, so this must be English territory," I reasoned.

Before leaving I paused in the main room to study a painting of Saint George spearing a dragon. Still lost in wonderment at the awesome mural, I headed out the door and glanced across the street to the Apollo Theater, where the marquee declared its current offering, a Cecil B. DeMille film called *"Reap the Wild Wind."*

"Man, wouldn't it be neat if Mr. DeMille shot a movie about Saint George?" I speculated. "Maybe if I write him a letter he'll do it. After all, Mr. DeMille is a graduate from P.M.C., right here on 14th Street. I wonder if Pop knew about Saint George when he laid hands on brother George's head and gave him that name? Well, if peeling potatoes at the Boyd Diner all night for a buck doesn't kill George, it just might turn him into a saint!"

These conjectures carried me to Zarnaski's Restaurant at the corner of Third and Lloyd. Looking in the window, I couldn't envision any coins crossing my palm. There was only one customer, and he was slouched at the table opposite the window, leaning over a bowl of beet soup loaded with sour cream. The checkered tablecloth was stained with a seeping purple spot and a big white splat. I almost entered the restaurant to give the poor guy a freebee, but the clock on the wall said 9:06, and I had a curfew to meet.

I decided to cross over Lloyd Street. A quick scan of the block told me it was strictly residential, and I was beginning to feel uneasy about the prospects of selling all my papers.

Crossing the street diagonally in a downcast mood, I decided to check the window of Molla's Flower Shop. I stood for a minute inhaling the aroma of the displayed roses: pink, yellow, red, arranged to perfection in dark-green urns. Closing my eyes, I imagined walking upstairs to Mom's room, coins in one hand and flowers in the other, catching the look of surprised joy on her face.

"One of these nights, I'll do just that!" I promised myself. "I'll splurge the whole night's take on roses!"

Walking away backwards with this resolution in mind, I stumbled on an uplifted crack in the pavement and landed unceremoniously on my hands and knees. Tree roots near the curbstone had done it. As I sat by the offending tree, nursing a scraped knuckle, a strolling neighborhood resident walked over, hoisted me up, grabbed a paper laying on the ground, handed me a dime, then walked away whistling.

"Hey, I stumble like a klutz, and I'm rewarded," I marveled. I started whistling my own little improvised ditty: *"Good things can happen to a good kid, and humbly speaking I'm one of the best."*

My whistling was way out of tune, due to a sliver of pear skin creviced between my front teeth. I finally dug it out with a fingernail while standing in front of the Chester Pharmacy near the corner of Pusey Street.

"Looks like another bleak block for me," I thought. "Nothing on this block but a hospital."

I was tempted to walk inside the pharmacy and ask for an emergency Band-Aid, but the pharmacist might slap some iodine on my knuckle instead. I picked up my pace. A Mercy Hospital nurse walked briskly down the cement pathway to the street, her starch-stiff uniform commanding respect. Next to Mom and my sisters, Mary and Vicky, I counted nurses among the most respected people on earth. But, then again, thoughts of my recent tonsillectomy at Chester Hospital flashed into my mind, along with a vision of the Angel of Mercy who had denied me water when I'd felt a post-surgery delirium that had been like crossing the Sahara Desert at noon.

Crossing Ulrich Street, I tried pronouncing the word *"Ulrich"* the way I'd heard the natives pronounce it before, and it didn't sound right. "Ul" as in "mull" and then "rich," but everyone says "Ull-rick."

"I'm in the seventh grade," I remarked to myself, "and I'm still confused about the English language. It's a good thing Pop and Mom got together and told us 'We are in America now; we speak only English with you children.' English is confusing enough; the sounds don't match the words. And if I'd picked up Pop's accent while he taught me how to speak Ukrainian, phew, I'd have to fight all around town every night!"

These mental pleasantries carried me across Ulrich Street to face the glass-encased announcement of weekly services at the Second Presbyterian Church.

"Boy! Presbyterians are serious people. They probably put a lot of money in the collection plate," I reasoned. "When they lay the foundation of a building, they really do a permanent job."

The glass-displayed message read:

JOIN US

IN WEEKLY PRAYER

FOR OUR TROOPS.

GOD BLESS AMERICA

Like a proudly worn badge, the invitation was there for all who happened to walk by. Thoughts shifted to the Russian Ukrainian Baptist Church I attended each Wednesday and twice on Sunday. (If I "hookied" church and Pop got wind of it, there were consequences.) Our church had once been a home, with the interior walls removed to create a sanctuary. It was small; 10 strides would carry me from back to front. A carpeted center aisle separated two sections of fold-down wooden chairs that squeaked when restless kids squirmed around. The pulpit and the semi-grand piano swallowed up most of the carpet-covered platform, upon which Reverend Bartkow and Connie Lemko would lead worship services. The wall behind the pulpit was adorned with Cyrillic letters, spelling out the Bible verse John 3:16.

It was from this platform that golden words and spirited music sounded to challenge a growing awareness of who I was: a child of God born to carry the name David Komarnicki. The answer to "Why am I here?" was beginning to come clear to me. I was placed on earth to learn to love God, family, and my neighbor as I love myself.

My sister Mary, the eldest child and budding family historian, had told me that our family lived on the second floor of the church before I was born. Brother George was born there, and brother Dan almost died there. When I came along, our family of 10 crowded the three bedrooms, and so Pop and Mom and their brood had moved on.

As I stood there on the sidewalk fronting the Second Presbyterian Church, feeling the moisture of the night air, suspended somewhere between reverie and reality, I glanced down at the headlines of the newspapers I was peddling.

"American kids just a couple of years older than me are dying on the beaches of Italy," I thought sadly, "kids from this neighborhood, maybe kids from churches on this street. And this Sunday, neighbors will kneel and pray for God to bless America. They'll ask Him to bless the troops cramped in foxholes, running scared on beaches—beaches meant for running in the sand, riding the surf, floating in patched inner tubes. Please, God, bring them home to have kids—kids like me, kids happy to bring nickels and dimes home to catch the reward of their Mom's smile before they trot off to bed."

These thoughts circulated behind misty eyes as I walked on to peek through the curtained window of DiMeglio's Restaurant. Again, not a remote chance of a sale. There was only one person inside—maybe the owner? He was a forlorn, pear-shaped man, coffee cup lifted to his parted lips, left hand scratching his bushy, jet-black hair. The color reminded me of the black shoe polish kept in the rear panel of my shoeshine box.

As I walked away from the window, I thought about a miscue I'd made the previous Saturday afternoon when a customer had his foot propped atop my box, ready for a shine. Judging from his dapper appearance, I'd felt a big tip was imminent.

Just as I'd straddled my box about to apply the polish to his fashionable Florsheim, an ear-piercing blast had attacked my sensitive cochlea. It was Officer Kandravi blowing the whistle on me! As his slow jog closed the ground between us, I'd considered my sparse options. Splotching my customer's elegant cardigan sock with black polish in my haste, I'd scooped up my box and taken off, imploring him to wait until I got back. He'd looked at his sock, then at me, in disbelief.

"Kandravi has foiled me again!" I'd moaned as I ran the two-and-a-half-block circuit around the Pennsy Railroad Station. When I returned, my customer was already halfway down Edgmont Avenue.

As I recalled the shameful event, I realized that I

really couldn't blame Officer Kandravi. He was only enforcing the law recently passed by City Council, saying that shoe-shining on public thoroughfares was henceforth deemed illegal, with exception for "Licensed Parlors."

"Why us independents?" I wondered. "I guess it's because the city can't keep tabs on the cash money that kids make and can't charge a tax on it. Boy, I love the fancy words they use when ordinances are posted in the *Chester Times,* words like HENCEFORTH and THOROUGHFARES."

When I'd read about that latest ordinance, I thought about all the cigar-chewing politicians strutting through town, sporting three-piece suits bought at John McGovern's Men's Shop. I'd set pins for those men at the Penn Bowling Alley and carried scars from pins bouncing of my shinbones while they tossed a dime tip down the alley and thought it was a big deal. I'd watched them taking their ease in the leather-cushioned chairs at the Republican Club on Welsh Street, blowing smoke rings across the room.

"Someday I'll make enough money to match their Christmas Club accounts at the Delaware County National Bank," I vowed. "How many times have I stood curbside, watching as they wave at voters from plush convertibles inching up Edgmont Avenue in the Fourth of July Parade? Did any of them ever shine shoes on a Saturday afternoon when they really wanted to play baseball in Deshong Park?"

I doubted it. And here I was, facing the rain and trying to add to the family income because my big brothers were away fighting for our country, A few days ago, I'd blotched the sock of a Big Tipper because I had to run away from a cop who couldn't catch me in a phone booth—all because politicians stacked the deck against kids trying to make a buck in exchange for honest labor.

113

I was so fumed I spit on the sidewalk. In fact, I ran out of spit as I walked right by Quattro's Tavern. Swallowing my political ill will, I retraced my steps, grabbed the entry door, and—whammo!—I was slammed against the wall by a short, stocky, bald-headed man barreling past me. His wife, her head wrapped in a babushka, was right behind him, steering the breadwinner home with what remained of his week's wages. While the man raged on in a Slavic monologue, the wife trod silently three steps behind at curbside—a protective sheep-herding move in case her inebriated husband stumbled into traffic.

Reopening the door, I stepped into the barroom, sized up my next maneuver, and made a beeline for the backroom, lured there by a mood-meister tickling the ivories for patrons arranged in a semicircle around a cushioned rail.

Easing into the room, I was suddenly caught up in the lyrical mood of "My Funny Valentine." The pianist eyed me standing there as I lip-synched the lyrics. He slid into a chord pattern and waved me forward to stand beside him.

Offering me the microphone, he whispered in a raspy Louie Armstrong voice, "Can you take it from the top, kid?"

Such moments seldom happen in life, so with a flair probably inherited from brother John, whose impromptu spirit had lodged early in my bosom, I placed my newspapers by my right foot and accepted the mike. Facing the intimate audience horseshoeing the piano, I took feathered flight into the Rodgers & Hart lyrics:

My funny Valentine
Sweet comic Valentine
You make me smile with my heart
Your looks are laughable, unphotographable

Yet you're my favorite work of art

Is your figure less than Greek?
Is your mouth a little weak?
When you open it to speak, are you smart?

But don't change a hair for me
Not if you care for me
Stay little Valentine, stay
Each day is Valentine's Day

Clapping, whistles, and bravos followed. Then, reaching for my inventory on the floor, as if bowing in response to their applause, I straightened up in time to see the pianist lift a dollar bill from his tip bowl on the piano, then place it in my hand as a professional courtesy. The receptive audience followed his lead with quarters— some for papers, others strictly for my impromptu performance. Intoxicated by my brief foray into show business, I worked the bar, selling *Inquirers* as I shuffled my way to the exit.

Once outside, my spirit soared in spite of the cold rush of rain drizzle. The air tingled in my lungs as my well-worn summer sneakers touched down like cat's paws on the shimmering cement sidewalk. I could have levitated, but my bulging pocketful of coins grounded me. Crossing Kerlin Street diagonally, I paused to allow a Buick roadster with a Delaware license plate to pass as it pulled out of the corner service station. The driver ignored the stop sign, then tossed a crumpled cigarette wrapper out of his rolled-down window. I stooped to pick it up as he sped west toward Marcus Hook.

"Thanks, Mr. X," I said to myself. "I'll peel off the silver paper and add it to my collection for the war effort, but it's idiots like you that trash neighborhoods while keeping your own ashtray clean."

I spit on the sidewalk again while plodding toward

downtown Chester. My inventory was still way too heavy, and Mr. Berman's demand for zero returns echoed in my ears.

"Would Mr. Berman really give this nightly route to another kid, maybe even Tony DeSantis?" I wondered. It was a troubling thought, and it harassed me like a green-eyed horsefly.

I doubled my pace as I crossed Parker Street, but I was immediately stopped cold by the candy displayed in Deakyne's Confectionery window. The sight of all those boxes of chocolates, caramels, bonbons, almonds, and peanut brittle started my mouth-juices jangling, but the imagined sweetness made my tongue curl instinctively to the crater on the right side of my gum line. Sobering memories of Dr. Mielcarek's pliers put an end to my droolings, and I pacified my sweet tooth with my last stick of Wrigley's Spearmint.

I moved on to Petrillo's Tavern, entered, scanned the room for indications of interest, and caught the bartender's backhanded wave calling me to the open end of the bar. He took a coin from the register, patted me on the head, then dropped his hand—which had magically become a clenched fist with a nickel wedged between its knuckles.

I grinned, pinched the nickel from between his fingers, and thanked him. "Will you teach me how to do that sometime?"

"Sure, kid, come back when it's not busy," he said with a friendly smile.

Across the bar a happy drunk with a front tooth missing was inhaling enough hops and lager to warrant his sleeping there tonight. I said goodbye to the bartender, feeling I'd made a friend—which was a good thing, because bartenders had a lot of clout in this newspaper-hustling business.

Dashing across the street, I headed for the Abruzzi Club but paused before opening its heavy mahogany door. I wanted to focus my thoughts before entering.

"Sometimes you've got to be ready, like walking on stage," I said to myself. "You've got to bounce in with alacrity, fervency, and spirit."

Taking a quick glance at the newspaper headline, I cleared my throat, adjusted my voice to a command-attention level, then entered shouting, "GI's drive Nazis out of Salerno! GI's drive Nazis out of Salerno!"

Nearly a dozen papers changed hands in less than a minute. A silver-haired, fatherly man with sad eyes invited me to help myself to the sandwich spread laid out on two tables covered with white tablecloths along the far wall of the dining room. The kingly feast featured every Italian delicacy this side of Rome.

I smiled, accepted his offer, and then proceeded to concoct a sandwich big enough to challenge a horse's jaw span. My brother Dan had once told me, "Never refuse hospitality, especially if they think you speak the language."

With that timely remembrance, I responded with a loud "grazie." I found an out-of-the-way table, wary perhaps that a local member of City Council might spot me, then cite an Abruzzi by-law declaring the feeding of urchin paperboys not domiciled in the ward to be hereby deemed illegal. It took 15 minutes to *mangia mangia* that Italian delight. I thanked my sad-eyed *gumba* and then departed with a muted burp of gratitude for Abruzzi hospitality.

Continuing east on Third Street, I paused while passing the Italian Presbyterian Church.

"Wow, this is the second Presbyterian church I've passed on Third Street, not to mention the Episcopal

Church and Saint Anthony's down the street, but where are the Baptists churches?" I wondered.

As I walked on slowly, almost bumping into passers-by walking in the opposite direction, I conjured up visions of Pop sitting in the back row of our little Russian Ukrainian Baptist Church on Eighth Street, caught up in the rapture of a hymn, choking back tears as he sang in full baritone:

Jesus, Jesus,
How I trust him,
How I've proved him o'er and o'er
Jesus, Jesus, precious Jesus,
Oh, for faith to trust him more.

Pop delivered lyrics clear and strong, and they carried throughout that little cramped congregation, but his fervor had yet to reach the inner chambers of my 13-year-old heart.

Standing in the gathering mist, I suddenly realized that a family could live and die on this street and never have to leave the neighborhood. Mama could give birth at Mercy Hospital, walk Third Street daily to squeeze fresh fruits and vegetables for the evening meal. Papa could catch the bus to Sun Shipyard, Baldwin Locomotive, Sun Oil, Scott Paper, the Ford plant, Baldt Anchor, Westinghouse Electric, or Sinclair Oil, while Mama stayed home and took care of the family.

"Everything can be done or fixed on these few blocks," I reflected. "Kids can walk to Saint Anthony's Grammar School, and men can gather at the Abruzzi Club to talk business or politics, shoot pool, and rehash memories of the old country. Down the street are the post office, the bakery, the florist, and the shoemaker. The money is safe in the Italian Bank, weddings are held at the Columbus Center, and there are funeral parlors to pay respects in times of greatest need. Birth to death and everything in between."

A bus stopped at the corner of Fulton Street, and I watched a debonair gentleman step down. He stood at attention as his well-appointed lady disembarked, then took her elbow and attentively supported her short walk to the curbstone. With a backward wave, he called out "Arrivederci!" to the bus driver.

"I'm walking the streets of Little Italy, woven right into the patchwork quilt of Chester," I told myself. "Their language is opera to my ear, and even though I can't say anything except hello, goodbye, and thank you, I'm accepted like a native son."

Passing the Italian Bank, I crossed the street and entered Joe's Tavern, where my ear was greeted with the voice of a true *paisano*, Frank Sinatra, crooning "My Blue Heaven" while locals, standing two deep at the bar, exhaled clouds of smoke thicker than you'd find at an all-night poker game. Burning eyes and a queasy gut forced me to exit before I could unload any of my papers.

I stepped outside to recuperate, inhaled rain drizzle along with the fresh air, and promptly succumbed to chesty heaves that doubled me forward to a fetal position. I straightened up in time to catch sight of Tony DiSantis, my chief competitor, stepping into the Italian American Club: "NUTS! Now what? That was my next stop. Competition lurks everywhere," I grumbled to myself.

I broke into a slow trot so I could put some space between us before he finished working the room. Tony had been coming from the direction I was heading in, and I wondered if he'd already hit the places I was planning to visit on my way toward town. I added that distressing thought to my list of worries, which already included Mr. Berman's command to sell out, the pending ten o'clock curfew, the drizzle about to burst into full-fledged rain,

119

the crouching dogs, and the lurking thieves. Suddenly the kid in the poolroom flashed into my mind, running a rack, one ball at a time—focused, unconcerned about who watched him. Speaking of focus, I had to focus on unloading the rest of my papers.

Just then, the Chester Police paddy wagon rolled by. A policeman stood on the rear runner, one hand holding the steel hand-grip, the other on his billy club. The disturber of the peace sat inside, leaning over, elbows on knees, no doubt trying to figure out how to explain his plight to his wife and kids.

A sudden shiver of remembrance surfaced through the drizzle. I could see clearly the day that same paddy wagon hauled me and three of my buddies off to the police station. They'd nailed us for playing tag football in the Quaker graveyard on Edgmont Avenue. Without warning, they'd stormed the graveyard, confiscated our football, and loaded us into the double-parked wagon. The police had then driven slowly up Market Street, as if on parade for all gawkers to get a good look.

The fact that it was my first recorded offense ... and the fact that Billy Lykens's father, a friend of the family, was a cop ... and the fact that Detective Ryan lived around the corner on Crosby Street ... and the fact that I had five older brothers and most cops in town knew them ... and the fact that none of my brothers had a police record that I knew of ... and the fact that none of the cops were Quakers might be a partial reason why the incident had never reached the court docket. They'd let us go scot-free but had made us squirm in the police station for a couple of hours, reflecting on all that would happen when we got home.

While sitting, I'd overheard one of the cops talking to his partner in a horse whisper, "That kid's dad is the best cook in town, works at the Boyd Diner. I get the blue plate special there for 35 cents."

120

I'd left the police station feeling that the system has a soft spot for kids and also that it was helpful for a kid to have a family with a good name.

Crossing Franklin Street, I couldn't see any action on this block either, only a half-dozen people in DiLucido's restaurant, so I stood resting for a while, leaning on a parking meter and looking up and down the street. Across the street stood Saint Anthony's Church, where an older couple had just opened the door to enter the sanctuary.

"This is where neighbors should be tonight," I thought. "They should be here praying on bended knee for victory in the war instead of drowning their misery in the taprooms."

Just then a Pileggi & Sons truck eased away from the curb as I stepped onto the drizzle-slick street. There wasn't really any reason to cross the street, so I headed toward Concord Avenue, wondering if Tony DiSantis had gotten to the Chelsea Hotel and Bar before me. Crossing my fingers, I entered. Luck prevailed. I unloaded four papers at the bar and then stood alongside the jukebox listening to Perry Como suture the wounds of the lonely with "Blue Moon":

Blue Moon, you saw me standing alone,
Without a dream in my heart
Without a love of my own
Blue Moon, you knew just what I was there for
You heard me saying a prayer for
Someone I really could care for

What I was "there for" was to sell papers. Today was my 13th birthday, and I was born with an ear for music. Even at my age, I felt the sentimental loneliness in the lyrics that Perry Como crooned. The tavern was packed. The smoke hung thicker than Mom's pea soup. The jukebox was a little too loud, but who'd complain? I walked the room, feeling like an unwelcome distraction. The patrons had come here to forget the war, a reality they had no power to change. I worked my way toward the exit as another Como classic dropped into play:

Alone from night to night you'll find me,
Too weak to break the chains that bind me,
I need no shackles to remind me,
I'm just a prisoner of love!

I lingered for a moment, watching the mustached bartender move like a maestro, orchestrating bottle slides, shaking mixed drinks, while he crooned in tune with Perry:

She's in my dreams awake or sleeping,
Upon my knees to her I'm creeping,
My very life is in her keeping,
I'm just a prisoner of love . . .

"You should be home in bed, kid," said a fatherly looking man, breaking into my lyric-induced trance.

"Got to sell all my papers, sir, before I go home," I retorted.

He bought two, giving me a quarter for them, patted me on the head, and said, "Hope this helps."

"Thanks, mister," I said with a grateful grin.

Taking fresh heart, I shuffled my way across the floor toward the back booths, secondhand cigar and cigarette smoke burning my eyes and finding each open pore of my body. On the hardwood dance floor, three couples were moving in tandem as Perry Como continued to open the floodgates of pent-up feelings:

What's the good of my caring,
If someone is sharing those arms with me?
Although she has another,
I can't have another for I'm not free.

I departed reluctantly, walking into the drizzle with a lighter load, some added cash, and smoke-clouded eyes. I felt privy to a timeless longing of the heart, my own uninitiated heart as well as the heart of the world. The sway of Perry Como's lyric poetry excited an itch I had not yet learned how to scratch. The dancers were loosening the cares of the war with music, while the bar crowd drank their mind-numbing brew, all of them trying to forget the chaos of the world.

This reverie almost got me hit by passing traffic as I jaywalked backwards onto Third Street, edging between two parked cars. I paused at the corner of Penn Street to rest, balancing my load of newspapers atop a fire hydrant. The streetlight cast an eerie spider web reflection on the misty street, created by its shattered dome.

"Could this be evidence of an accurate slingshot or the tossed rock of an ingrate, or could it be the work of a Red Rider BB gun?" I mused.

Looking down Penn Street through the mist flooding in from the Delaware River, I could hear the baleful warning sound of a tugboat claiming its space as it moved through the fog. The drizzle was getting serious as I picked up the pace towards Dock Street, and I slowly became aware that a sense of neighborhood was becoming lost as I moved along. I noticed a dead cat laying in the gutter directly in front of Mazza's Café, and I took it as a bad omen and kept moving.

I wasn't much on superstitious stuff, but I had strong feelings that things were not exactly right on this block, so I kept looking around and walking fast until I entered the Anchor Café. A quick glance around the room warned me that I was potentially in harm's way.

I approached a seedy-looking man with a stubbled face, who was parked in a booth along the far wall, slouching over a headless mug of beer. He shot me a sardonic look when I timidly ventured, "Paper, mister?"

It was a "kidnapper look," the cold, measured stare of a loser who'd just as soon blackjack me in a dark alley, stuff me in his duffel bag, shoulder-carry me aboard a freighter, chain me in storage, and sell me for a six-pack in Hong Kong. He glared at me without comment, then eyeballed the Fort Knox of coins bulging in my pockets.

Easing towards the entrance, I checked to see if there was a side exit for Captain Hook to slip out and jump me, but there wasn't, so I cut through the smoke-filled room without breathing until I was safely outside. I then flew on cushioned arches toward the Third Street bridge. As I ran along the inclined curb, I could see rivulets of rain forming in the gutter and moving towards the sewer drain that emptied the run-off into the river. I hurried across the narrow bridge and walked curbside after crossing, wary of spaces between darkened storefront windows where misfits could be lurking.

I stood in the drizzling rain, facing the Pabst Blue Ribbon neon sign scrolling across the window of Keenan's Bar and Tavern, shielding my inventory of unsold papers with my hunched shoulders. Gaining entry to this bar wasn't easy. If spotted by Mr. Keenan, I'd get the boot. Normally, he shouted a one-word exclamation: "OUT!" And, if one was handy, he'd wave me toward the door with the flicker of a bar towel—a signal hard to ignore.

But tonight I had to chance it, feeling a renewed urgency to "sell out" with so few taverns remaining. I edged the plate glass door open just far enough to check Mr. Keenan's position. He normally tended to his drink disbursement behind the 20-foot bar running along the side wall. I was not a kid easily discouraged, so while his back was turned towards the entry door I slipped through in a crouch, advancing unseen to the rear where the raucous booth crowd sat imbibing.

The unbroken line of men at the bar shielded my crouched advance toward the back room. My knee-bending squat was noticed by all but Mr. Keenan. As I inched along, patrons at the bar thought I was a crippled kid doing my part for a poor family, so when I reached the back room in my halting crouch, the patrons unleashed a torrent of generosity with tips beyond the usual nickel. They handed me quarters and smiled me away with, "Keep it, kid." I sold five papers in five booths.

Just then Mr. Keenan caught sight of me, waving me out with his trusty bar towel. I stayed in a low crouch until the entry door closed behind me, but before the door closed I heard a guy at the bar holler, "Why so tough on the kid, Joe? Can't you see he's a cripple?"

Straightening up, I went out onto the street and walked to the corner. Glancing to the right, I looked through the misty rain into Commission Row, which in the early morning hours would be teeming with the city's grocers and restaurant-owners buying their fruit, vegetables, and fresh fish. A few more steps took me to the entrance of Minnetti's Bar. As soon as the door closed behind me, good fortune shone in the smile of the brunette barmaid.

"Look who just came out of the rain," she called out, holding out her arms to give me a hug.

She nodded her head toward two regulars, and they both waved me forward for quick sales. Along with the coins, I picked up a couple of head rubs. While pausing to tighten the shoelace of my sneaker, foot propped on the brass bar rail, I thought about how sweet it was to have a benefactor with enough influence to cause a hand to reach into a pocket and cough up a quarter for a newspaper. The hug was pretty sweet, too.

"If I ever grow up," I daydreamed, gazing at the barmaid. "If I ... ah, who cares about my ifs?"

I waved my thanks to her on the way out, then paused in the covered entry for traffic to clear before crossing to the City Hotel. A Goff's Seafood truck turned into Commission Row, perhaps to unload fresh fish for the next morning's wholesale crowd. I watched rain splattered by the windshield wipers of a Night Owl Fruit & Produce truck heading west on Third Street. Before tiptoeing across, I took note of which puddles hid the gaping potholes in the Belgium-block street.

I straightened my posture before opening the oak-and-glass entry door to the City Hotel. Scanning the well-appointed lobby, I walked quietly toward an occupied Morris chair planted on the fringe of a massive Oriental rug by the fireplace. What a happy surprise! It was my friend Luke Howard, sitting erect with the air of a journalist about to deliver an eyewitness account of his charge up San Juan Hill in tandem with Teddy Roosevelt. Luke Howard was a permanent fixture at the YMCA, and I'd often sat listening to his detailed accounts of the "good old days" before the Spanish-American War.

"Glad you showed up," he said. "Two kids were here already, but I turned them down, thinking you might be along at any minute."

As he talked on, he pinched a coin from an oval-shaped coin purse, and I handed back change—knowing that he lived on a tight pension. A glance at the wall clock showed that my curfew time was only 20 minutes away, so I had to cut the conversation short before Luke launched into one of his lengthy discourses.

I said, "Thanks, Luke, thanks for waiting for me. I'll see you at the Y."

He waved as I walked away, and I turned back to leave him with a parting expression of gratitude: "Someday, when I write about loyalty, I'll write an article about you, Luke."

126

He smiled and then unfolded the paper to read about a war he would have to sit out in a Morris chair.

A man heading for the bar spotted me, signaled me over, and bought a paper. His Stetson was angled to the right, and he had the demeanor of a bookie struggling to cover his bets. I followed him five paces behind into the bar. Upon entering, I spotted a quarter half-buried in the sawdust. Without breaking stride, I scooped it up.

"You can keep it for a trick or a newspaper," intoned a man wearing steel-toed work shoes.

I looked him in the eye and said, "You're talking Halloween, and this is still September, mister."

He had the no-nonsense look of a stevedore, so I backed away smiling. Not quite sure how to handle this challenge, I stuffed the quarter into my pocket— remembering at that exact second what a new kid at Larkin had hollered at me as he picked up my Tom-troller in an after-school marble game: "Possession is nine-tenths of the law!"

This kid was BIG and had great bully potential, but fewer things in life meant more to me than my Tom-troller. I'd called upon the reservoir of strength brother John had taught me to tap into, if and when needed, and had rammed that big kid against a giant acorn tree, then worked him over with the intensity I'd seen Johnny Fry demonstrate at Lloyd Field. With bloody nose cupped in one hand, he'd dug into his pocket with the other, returning my prize marble without a word.

Before departing, I'd given him one last blow, a verbal one: "If your Pop's a lawyer, tell him you had to cough up nine marbles to get home in time for supper. Your nine-tenths of the law business may work in the court house, but it won't work on the playground!"

With memories of my nose-bloodying revolt against

the law of possession circulating in my head, it suddenly occurred to me that the tables might be turned on me here in the back room of the City Hotel. Since I wasn't about to give up the quarter, I decided that I'd better fork over a paper.

I took the side exit out onto Edgmont Avenue and immediately ducked under the roofed, glass-sided entryway into Mercadante's Barber Shop to avoid the downpour. While waiting, I double-folded my last newspaper and tucked it under my hooded jacket before darting across the rain-slick street for my last stop of the evening. Lowering my head, I plunged across the street and almost canceled my ticket to life when a Bell Cab, racing through the now pelting rain, almost fendered me to kingdom come.

I kept on going, not looking back until I reached the Stanley Theater, my adrenaline still pulsing from the close shave with the cab. I calmed down by walking back and forth under the protective marquee that extended overhead to the street.

It was 9:50 p.m., perilously close to curfew, when I ducked into the Stanley Luncheonette next door. I was urged in by brother George's often repeated adage, "A treat a day keeps the blues away." I didn't understand the "blues" part, but, after all, today was my 13th birthday and I was determined to celebrate the occasion with a treat.

Lifting my last newspaper from under my sweatshirt, I tucked it under my arm and then opened the door. As the door clicked closed behind me, the counterman bellowed, "What paper you got there, kid?"

"The *Inquirer*," I replied, "but it's slightly wet. It's yours for two cents."

"I'll take it," he said. He fingered a liberty dime across the counter, and I smoothed out the wrinkled paper before handing it over the worn Formica countertop. I saddled the counter stool, then passed the dime back toward the counterman's chocolate-stained apron.

"Cherry Coke, please, no ice, two straws. And keep the dime, I'll want a refill."

As he fizzed the fountain Coke into a glass, I surveyed the nearly empty room. A soldier, sitting in a booth with his girlfriend, their heads almost touching, dropped a coin in the wall-mounted jukebox selector. Then, gazing into her eyes, he let Frank Sinatra express his sentiments:

I'll be seeing you
In all the old familiar places
That this heart of mine embraces
All day through...

The counterman, leaning forward, whispered to me, "The soldier just got in from boot camp, 13 weeks at Indiantown Gap."

Looking again, I noticed the soldier singing along with Frank. He and his girl rubbed noses, lost in the ecstasy of the moment.

The counterman, returning with my Coke, asked curiously, "Why two straws?"

"So I can taste on both sides of my tongue," I answered.

He shot me a quizzical look, then began combing the newspaper for the horseracing results. He stopped, focused, and then leaned over the paper with index finger pointed to the race result that he, by the look on his face, had lost. Suddenly, looking my way, he asked, "Are you a Komarnicki? Your face looks familiar."

"Yeah," I acknowledged, "and I probably look familiar because I look into your window almost every night when I'm peddling my papers. There are so few customers here that I move on. I've noticed that your neon light buzzes like a bee, and you lost the juice in the last four letters."

I wasn't trying to be smart. It was just a fact.

"Yeah, the theater crowd rushes in after the show breaks, but otherwise business is pretty sparse. Anyways, I know your brother Mickey—went to Smedley Junior High with him. I didn't see much of him at Chester High."

"Yeah, Mickey had to quit high school to help with the monthlies," I explained between sips. "He went to work with Pop at the Boyd Diner. He's in the Army now, though—joined up before he got drafted. Mickey never waited for things to happen. He's always been on the move."

Leaning on the counter, talking sideways to me while scanning the paper, he said, "Your brother Mickey sure made some smooth moves on skates at the Great Leopard. In fact, he was so smooth most skaters would clear the floor just to watch him and his girlfriend zip around the rink."

As the counterman went back to reading his paper, I thought about Mickey. "Right now, those legs aren't gliding around a skating rink," I said to myself. "They're walking muddy roads in Burma."

I watched my cherry Coke approach the bottom of my glass. How neat it was to hear a stranger tell me good stuff about my brother.

"Boy, my brothers sure paved a five-lane road right down the center of Chestertown for me," I thought. "A road smoother than a cement sidewalk. Wherever I touch down, I feel the fame and protection of our family name."

The counterman moved to the front door after

130

ringing up the tab for the couple caught in the pangs of love. He then double-bolted the door, posted the "Closed" sign, and returned to scrutinize the newspaper.

"I got a brother in the Army, too," he told me. "I think he landed with the troops in Salerno." He then made a sign of the cross from head to chest and whispered a short reflective prayer for the protection of his brother.

The sound of my empty straws draining the remnants of my cherry Coke broke the mood. The counterman turned, walked over, then lifted my glass for a refill. I propped both elbows on the counter, cleared my throat, and thanked him for buying my last newspaper, for the refill, and for sharing his memories of my brother Mickey.

"Hearing about him almost brings Mickey home," I thought. "I can almost hear his nimble feet touch down on every squeaky step as he spans them two by two to his third-floor room. But he's NOT there, not really, and while I sleep tonight he's backpacking his way across an ox-rutted road somewhere in Burma."

Looking at the friendly counterman, I decided to let him in on the reason I was treating myself to a Coke. "You know, this is a special occasion for me. Today's my 13th birthday."

He turned to look me full in the face, almost as if he could catch a reflection in my eyes of what he'd felt like when he was 13. He stared intently while wiping his fingers on his stained white apron. He then turned, as if in search of something. On the counter, in a glass display case, sat a single slice of Boston cream pie. He walked over, slid the door open, reached in, lifted out this culinary work of art, and placed it in front of me.

"Happy birthday, kid," he beamed at me. "Enjoy it. This is a salute to our brothers." He turned toward the back of the restaurant, looked over his shoulder, and said,

"Take your time, kid. I gotta clean up the kitchen."

And take my time I did—first savoring the chocolate overlay, then the yellow cream filling, flattening each delicious intake against the roof of my mouth. I felt the trickling luxury of cherry Coke wash the flavor past my vacant tonsil sockets.

"This odyssey on my 13th birthday will lodge in every cell of my being," I thought as I stared into my own face reflected in the mirror behind the counter.

When I finally walked to the door to leave, I paused to shake the counterman's hand. I thanked him for the pie and repeated my sentiments about the memory-gift about my brother Mickey. The door clicked shut behind me as I walked into the rain. I looked skyward, inviting the rain to dance on my uncovered head. This spontaneous baptism on my 13th birthday added confirmation to the good fortune of my life as I walked the two blocks to Sixth and Welsh to turn over $5 for the 250 papers Bobby Berman had entrusted me with.

I settled with Mr. Berman, and he let me keep the route. I was 45 minutes over curfew time, but Kandravi must have been snoring on his beat when I mounted the three granite steps to my front door. Lifting the door gently to soften the sound of the squeaky hinge, I eased in, walked the hallway to the foot of the stairs, and then gently called, "Mom, I'm home!"

As I climbed the stairs, heading up to the room I shared with Pop and three of my brothers, I caught sight of Mom's smile as she leaned over the banister with a large package half-hidden behind her back: "Happy birthday, David. I'm so glad you're home."

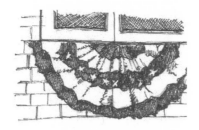

Independence Day, 1944

Anticipation was drifting drowsily through my early-morning slumber, when the unmistakable sound of a cherry-bomb exploding under a tin can jolted me awake. Loud laughter and the pungent smell of firecracker smoke drifted through my window, and a quick look outside confirmed that my neighbor Doodles and his cousin Harvey were the culprits. July 4, 1944, had begun with a bang.

I climbed into my clothes faster than a fireman late for a four-alarmer, then scurried down the backstairs to the kitchen. I kissed Mom on the forehead, emptied the Wheaties box into my bowl, and spooned its strength into my lean, 13-year-old body.

Today was the day Delaware County tilted toward Chester for the big Independence Day parade. The citizenry walked from Upland, bused from Media, and carpooled from Upper Darby, Lansdowne, Sharon Hill, Glenolden, Rutledge, Morton, and Marcus Hook— the pulsing blood of the county testing the capacity of Chester's heart.

Packed to the chin with the Breakfast of Champions and a hastily downed glass of orange juice, I headed out the door and sauntered up Seventh Street toward

133

Edgmont to soak up the festivities. The parade would form four blocks away at Third and Market, but the lunch-packing, Thermos-toting crowd had staked their claims early and were already three deep before starting time, stretched like a rubber band on Edgmont as far as I could see in both directions.

Only Kandravi the traffic cop seemed blissless as he stood waving traffic through the clogged artery at Seventh and Edgmont and whistling the steady stream of parade-goers onto the curb in front of Speare Brothers Department Store. Businesses had hung flags and draped bunting on every available pole, and the feeling of patriotic fervor was running high.

I walked along Edgmont toward Sixth Street, sure I'd find a space to slither into. I passed Speare's, Murray's, Birney's—no luck. I made my way to Sixth, thinking I'd climb the Pennsy Railroad embankment, but the Buckman Village kids had claimed the ledge, squatting where the incline allowed. As I emerged from the underpass, heading toward Fifth Street, a flock of nervous pigeons flew across the elevated tracks. They  flapped in loose formation, then circled to land on the roof of Kresge's Five and Ten Cent Store. Closing ranks, they formed a line as if they had reserved seats to catch the parade with an unimpeded view. And— WHACKO!—just like that, I knew what I would do.

Turning, I walked three steps to the Union News kiosk and bought five newspapers: a *Philadelphia Inquirer,* a *Philadelphia Record,* the *Public Ledger,* a *Bulletin,* and a *Chester Times.* Leon, the newsstand owner, looked a little puzzled as I forked over the 15 cents for the papers, since he knew I was a paper boy myself.

By the time I reached Whalen's Drug Store, the crowd had thickened to a pickpocket's delight. The clock in the store window said 9:30, which gave me 30 minutes until parade time. The sun was steadily rising in a cloudless sky, and sweat beads began popping out on collars and brows. Kids were everywhere—straddling their dads' shoulders, licking twin-stick orange popsicles, digging wooden spoons into Dixie cups, smearing their faces with cotton candy.

I maneuvered toward Fifth Street, my five newspapers locked under my left arm. As I walked along, I cataloged the names of the stores I passed, as if I had to know them all by heart: Cohen's Jewelry; Green's Market; McCoy's Men' Shop; Spencer's Stationery; Thom McCann's Shoes; Morris "Square Deal" Jewelers; Lloyd's Men's Shop; Freed's Furniture (where Freed himself was standing on one of his oak chairs so he could see over the crowd); Royal Shoes Market (my sisters would never grace this joint); Vogue Millinery (perhaps they'd window-shop here); Bomberger's Drug Store; and finally the Chester Cambridge Bank at the corner of Fifth and Market. Looming across the intersection was my destination—the Crozier Building, the tallest building in town.

My Joe Lapchick sneakers carried me nimbly across Fifth Street and swiftly negotiated the two white marble steps that led up to the majestic eight-story building. I pushed open the plate-glass doors and walked purposefully to the concession stand over near the elevator in the back corner of the lobby. The mingled aroma of Camels, Lucky Strikes, Chesterfields, and Muriel cigars immediately ganged up on my tender lung tissue.

"Pack of spearmint, please," I told the sales lady who sat atop a high stool. Plunking my nickel down on the counter, I thanked her and moved aside to open the pack and unwrap the first stick from its silver paper. I carefully folded it, inserted it in my salivating mouth, and then licked the sugary residue from my fingers.

Just then the elevator doors opened, and I stepped in with assurance. Face forward, I inched steadily backwards as others entered to cramp my space. A woman the size of a newborn hippo came in first, edging me toward a corner as we were joined by a couple wearing the etched frowns of a lifelong argument. A lawyer type stepped in next—decked out in a navy-blue, vested shantung suit, cuff-linked white shirt, and cordovan-polished Florsheims.

The hippo lady had me cornered until she waddled out on the fifth floor, producing a noticeable easement on the elevator cables. The frowning couple stepped out on the sixth floor, moving like two convicts joined by leg irons. Before making his exit on the seventh floor, the lawyer adjusted tie, cuffs, and collar as if answering a curtain call. Not one word had been spoken by any of us while we'd been on the rise.

Traveling to the eighth floor in brief but welcome solitude, I stepped out over the brass Otis signature plate on the metal threshold. Thanking Otis for the invention that had lifted the world into vertical integration and now potentially allowed me to observe the parade from a pigeon's vantage point, I turned right and headed toward the roof exit at the rear of the building.

I had to admit I'd been dreaming and scheming this moment since I'd first walked down Market Street. And walked it I had. At the age of five I'd walked with sister Mary to the foot of Market to board the Wilson Line for an excursion to River View Beach, that sandy paradise nestled downriver on the Jersey side at Pennsville. At the age of seven I'd walked unattended down Market to Third, where I'd unloaded Christmas-gift fantasies in Santa's ear at Stotter's Department Store. I'd walked it with Pop to visit his clubfooted friend Sam Douglas, from whom he bought the Bible tracts he'd later distribute to the sick at Chester, Taylor, and Crozer hospitals.

Now at the age of 13, I was finally on my way to the top of the city's tallest edifice. As I walked down the long, white-tiled hallway, about to test the limits of my loosely constructed conscience, I kept my newspapers securely tucked under my arm—an added cover in case anyone stepped out of one of the long line of offices to inquire as to my business on the eighth floor. If challenged, I'd simply say, "Paper, mister? I'm down to my last *Inquirer, Record, Ledger, Bulletin,* or *Chester Times.*"

As I moved down the long corridor, I passed "John McClure/Insurance," "Aaron Tollin, Esquire," "Joseph DeFuria, Esquire," "Chester Merchants Association," "John Hancock/Insurance," and "Lindsay Law Library," but none of the illustrious occupants emerged from behind their pebbled-glass doors. With one quick backward glance, I pushed the crossbar of the door marked "Roof Exit" and stepped onto the fire escape leading up to the roof.

I scrambled up quickly, without looking down through the corrugated steps to the alley eight floors below. Crossing onto the roof, I gingerly walked the catwalk toward the front of the building. At roof's edge I leaned forward on the chest-high guardrail, giving any gawkers down below the vicarious thrill of vertigo. I set my papers down, gave a quick salute to the pigeons lined up across the street on Kresge's rooftop, then did a slow 360-degree turn to drink in a panoramic sweep of the city. Gazing down on the Delaware River five short blocks away, my eyes zoomed in on a tugboat. Rubber tires were tied along the bow, serving as bumpers when nudging massive cargo ships into docking position. An oil tanker with a bellyful of crude cruised toward Sun Refinery. Turning northeast, I saw the Philadelphia skyline shimmering in the glare of the sun, William Penn standing jauntily atop City Hall.

I checked out the Port of Philadelphia, crowded with ships. I knew that heavily muscled stevedores were at work down there—wielding big metal hooks to steer cargo onto pallets for loading or unloading the bowels of the vessels. I knew this because my big brother John was a stevedore before he'd gone off to war, and he'd let me handle his hook once.

I followed the curved shoreline south. It was crammed with industries grinding out endless production to bury the enemy and end the war. Westinghouse was building generators; Sun Shipyard was launching cargo ships, one a week; Scott Paper was turning pulp into the best paper products on earth. Baldt Anchor, Sinclair Oil, and Sun Oil were arrayed along the shore, chimneys pointing heavenward, belching gray smoke and doing their best to blot out the morning sun. If an acrid smell and burning eyes were the result, so be it—if it helped defeat the enemy and bring my brothers home.

The river glistened in the baking summer sun, with foamy wakes trailing the ship traffic. Could this be the spot where William Penn first stepped ashore to walk among the Brotherhood of Friends? I looked down on the jostling crowd lined up in front of the Colonial Courthouse. That's where Sir William had signed the first colonial charter and later held the first Supreme Court in the American colonies.

Next my eye fell on the extended wooden awning next door, belonging to the Washington House Tavern where George Washington had rested his weary frame and logged his journal entries about the lost battle at Brandywine 14 miles south. I was deep in thought about General Washington scratching his quill pen across his diary pages when the shrill whistle of the Grand Master snapped the lead band into a drum-rolling high-step that brought a roar from the crowd below. The parade had begun.

I leaned over the tubular railing as far as faith would allow and thrilled to the brash, brassy sounds of the instruments and the chest-high prancing of the majorettes. Right behind the lead band came the veterans of World War I, shuffling along as fast as they could manage to a tune from their glory days:

Over there, over there
Send the word, send the word,
Over there
That the Yanks are coming,
The Yanks are coming,
The drums rum tumming everywhere
So prepare,
Say a prayer
Send the word,
Send the word to beware
We'll be over, we're coming over.
And we won't be back till it's over over there

The veterans extended their flags high, and kids perched on their dads' shoulders waved miniature flags back at them from curbside. Up on the roof, I snapped to attention with heels locked, standing like a one-man reviewing station as the parade moved steadily up Market. Units formed at Third and Market Square came to life with whistle and drum roll and began strutting to the waves of family and friends.

From eight stories up I could barely make out the embroidered lettering on the street-wide banners held chest-high by the various groups to announce the name of their society, their reason for being: "The Sons of Civil War Vets," "Spanish American War Vets," "The Veterans of Foreign Wars." They all moved with dignity and purpose, as if they were carrying their legacy with each step. They seemed to be moving down the street in memory of buddies left behind. Here came the American Legion, then the American War Mothers dressed in white, the Boy Scouts and Girl Scouts, the Grand Army of the Republic, the Jewish War Vets—all getting their big fat say on this warm sunny day.

An unforeseen pause in the action came when the mounted-police brigade was passing Fourth Street. Right in front of the Delaware County National Bank, a horse reared up on its hind legs, causing the curbed crowd to pull back in alarm. While the recalcitrant steed was calmed, one of his stable mates unloaded a giant pile of you-know-what right over a manhole cover. The crowd roared with laughter as the whole parade came to a halt for a manure-grabber to excavate the generous pile and cut down Fourth with the steaming treasure. During the break in the action, traffic cops opened up Fifth Street for vehicles to proceed through.

The parade resumed with the Knights of Malta, followed by a group whose banner read, "Artisans of Mutual Protection." (If school hadn't been out for the summer, I'd be asking Miss Eachus about that one in history class!)

On and on they came: gleaming fire engines; bald-headed bigwigs in late-model convertibles; Mayor Peoples flashing his toothy Roosevelt smile from the back of a Cadillac; baton twirlers who tossed their sticks skyward and caught them to the unanimous amazement of the crowd; and Chester's pride and joy, the high school band in their orange and black capes. The community was standing three deep, neighbor to neighbor, caught up in the electric mood as the parade kept on streaming up Market Street. From my rooftop perch I watched until the last band disappeared beneath the Pennsy Railroad underpass, heading for the Chester Rural Cemetery where local dignitaries would pay ceremonial homage to the fallen.

Eager to hear the solemn words that would mark the end of the festivities, I descended from the roof and exited the Crozier Building as fast as my 13-year-old legs would carry me. I quickly sold my five hastily purchased papers among the dispersing members of the crowd, then fell into step with the hardier folk who were following the parade all the way to the graveyard a mile away. Among the marchers I noticed Walter Budnick, whose brother Joe had been killed at Anzio Beach while running a message for his pinned-down unit.

Content to trundle along at the tail end of the crowd, I fell into a semi-trance as I thought of Joe in the simple scenes he'd never again enjoy. I remembered how he smiled so attentively as he watched Walter and another brother, Morris, singing in quartet with Danny and Paul Bartkow in our little Ukrainian church on Eighth. As the parade paused at the intersection of Seventh and Edgmont to let traffic go by, I recalled an image of Joe vaulting up the YMCA steps, heading for a workout. Another memory hit me—a church picnic where Joe, tied at the ankle with Danny Bartkow, competed in a three-legged race, cheered on by his sister Helen.

Joe had been good at every sport he tried, and I'd often stood in the alley behind the Madison Methodist Church, watching him take set-shots at the peach basket pinned to a pole until dusk called us both home to supper.

The parade moved on, marching by Deshong Park, and I had a vision of Joe rounding first base with a triple in mind. His speed was awesome.

No more triples, Joe, but you'll never run out of my memory.

The brass bands launched into a fervent rendition of "The Star-Spangled Banner" as we crossed the B & O track at 12th Street. At 14th we passed Imschweiler's Funeral Home, a silent sentinel of life's brevity.

141

The high-stepping ceased as the procession passed through the wrought iron archway of Chester Rural. All of us, the marchers and the crowd of followers, instinctively came together into a semicircle and fell into a respectful silence as the city fathers gave forth with speeches noting sacrifices made by soldiers since Revolutionary times. Flowers were placed on graves, and then a clergyman stepped forward to utter a prayer that God in His mercy would look kindly upon all who laid down their lives and that we who remained would live lives worthy of the sacrifices made.

The ceremony was over, and I headed home, thinking about everything I'd seen and remembered that day. When I reached our house, I stood across the street for a moment—leaning on a phone pole and looking at the five-star banner that hung in our window. I felt both sadness and gladness welling up in me.

Sadness for the death of Joe Budnick on a beach in Italy. Sadness for the fact I might never see my brothers again. But gladness that Mom and Pop lived by faith, spoon-fed me hope, and nurtured me in love every day of my life.

A Night to Remember

Major events happen seldom in life, but the night that a thousand butterflies took flight in my stomach I sensed one was about to happen.

It was a crisp Friday evening around Halloween when I eased into Charlie Peck's Ice Cream Emporium and commanded, "A hand-packed pint of peach, Mr. Peck, and please pack it tight ... a celebration treat for my mom."

Charlie complied with a smile. As he dipped, I counted out the coins for payment.

Stepping outside with Mom's treat in hand, I nudged the door shut with my left foot and gazed heavenward to check Orion's position in the clear October sky. Perfect, just where it should be this time of year, I reflected. I

143

stepped curbside between two parked cars, a black 1938 Packard and a pea-green Buick, both with an "A" gas-ration sticker on the window. Checking traffic both ways, I maneuvered an angled crossing on the uneven Belgium-block cobblestones of East Seventh Street.

Reaching the sidewalk in front of my house, I paused and stood at attention. I focused on the family's symbol of pride: an embroidered blue banner that featured five stars and hung in our front window, back-dropped by our frayed and faded window shade. I whispered a prayer for my off-to-war brothers: Mickey, walking the Burma Road; John, riding the fickle waves somewhere in the South Pacific; Joe, testing the untried limits of an Air Force plane; Dan, dreaming of Mom's pot roast while he languished at the Great Lakes Naval Training Base; and brother-in-law Richard (included among the brothers), somewhere near the White Cliffs of Dover, scribbling a V-mail to sister Vicky without revealing censorable secrets.

Mounting the three granite steps that made up our front stoop, I opened the door, traversed the hallway, danced up the 12 stairs, paused on the small square landing, turned right, and smiled my way into Mom's room, my hands thrust behind my back. Mom sat on the bed, awaiting my return from my nightly hustling of *Philadelphia Inquirers* in the local bars and restaurants.

"I sold out early tonight, Mom. The Beer Gardens were packed. I guess they're hungry for news about the war." I whispered to her, "Pick one, Mom."

It took only seconds for her to choose between my right hand and my left, but in those seconds the slanting hallway light revealed the anticipation in her eyes and framed the childlike innocence of her face.

She pointed to my left hand, and I placed the ice cream box beside her hip.

"Now put your palms together," I instructed. She

clasped her work-worn hands in front of her chest and watched in amazement as I poured nickels, dimes, quarters, and half-dollars into her upturned palms.

Her smile was reward enough for a 14-year-old breadwinner.

I perched on the bed beside her. "Remember what tonight is, Mom? It's celebration night. Tonight I sleep in Johnny's and Mickey's room."

"It's ready," she whispered back. "Clean sheets and your favorite quilt."

I hugged her tight and placed a light kiss on her right temple (my favorite spot), then vaulted down the hallway to the bathroom. After brushing my teeth, washing face and neck, and toweling down, I tugged open the bottom drawer of the old dresser in the corner and pulled out my stowed stack of comic books, wrapped in a "borrowed" YMCA towel and saved especially for tonight's celebration.

Retracing my steps, I passed Mom's room and noticed my youngest brother, Jim, propped next to her and sharing her prized treat. I paused at the half-open door of the bedroom I was vacating. Pop was already sleeping, imploding then exploding his lips in a rhythmic snore. Across the room, Paul was peacefully asleep in his half of the bed, unaware that Jim had snuck out for a late-night treat.

Turning left, I faced the 12 splintery steps that led upward to FREEDOM. I sprinted up to the top landing. To my left was George's new room (formerly occupied by Joe and Dan), and to the right was my new domicile, the former roosting place of my two oldest brothers. From the doorway, I surveyed this sanctum as if for the first time, even though it was the exact duplicate of the one below where I'd shared a squeaky bed with brother George for the past three years. His sleep had often included dreams of drop-kicking winning goals, and my calf muscle had often been used as the football.

Entering my new room, I dropped my towel-wrapped literary bundle on top of the lamp table, then took off shoes, socks, shirt, and Levis and let them lie in a heap bedside (readily available in case of a fire). I eased myself onto the bed, where Mom, true to her promise, had spread my favorite quilt. I extended my arms and legs, angling them to reach both sides of the mattress at once. Whoa! Whoa! Whoa! I couldn't finger or toe either edge! I was spread-eagled with room to spare. No more inter-twangled legs. No more knuckles in the night.

I lay there, scanning the room, listening for sounds stored in the cracked plaster walls—echoes left by Mickey and Johnny. Locked in my listening trance, I squinted my eyes, and, sure enough, I could hear it: the slow, methodical rumble of a 6-ounce coke bottle rolling back and forth, back and forth, on the pocked linoleum floor, the sound of Mickey's nightly rehab routine to strengthen torn ankle ligaments. And then another sound joined the chorus: the muted, exhaled grunts of John in route to his 100 nightly push-ups.

Sliding nimbly off the bed, I unwrapped my comic classics, then stuffed the towel along the bottom of the closed door to keep the light from bleeding into the stairwell just in case Pop decided to make a night visit to the bathroom. You learn a lot from five older brothers, I mused, as I tiptoed back to bed. I slid between the sheets, fresh from the clothesline of our postage-stamp patch of a yard, fluffed the pillows, and purred with catlike contentment. Making a random reach into my treasure trove, I pulled out a Captain Marvel and —SHAZAM!!!— I was glued to the storyline from the first page.

Just as the action between Captain Marvel and his archenemy, Sirvana, was coming to a white-knuckle climax, I saw the unthinkable: my pilfered YMCA towel was moving inward across the floor, and there, in the doorway, stood Captain Pop. Grave of countenance and silent as a stone, he advanced—a warrior of tough love, clad in the humble armor of white T-shirt and knee-length boxer shorts. His mute gaze bored right through to my conscience, where there was a lever labeled "Liberty or License." The look in Pop's eyes convinced me I'd flipped the lever in the wrong direction tonight. Without a word, he gathered up my treasured hoard, then departed in stony silence, taking with him all my envisioned evenings of literary pleasure.

Still in shock over the silent raid, I crawled out of bed and crept out into the hallway, just in time to see Pop reach the bottom of the back stairwell and step into the kitchen. Having two sets of stairs had come in handy on more than one occasion, and I wasted no time in taking advantage of the front-stairs route to the first floor, where I could see for myself what fate Pop had in store for my cherished collection.

Before I was even close to a spot where I could peek into the kitchen, the clang of the circular lid atop our coal stove gave me the first dreaded clue. Then I heard a series of sharp thrusts, as all 25 comic books were fed to the embers. I heard another clang as Pop replaced the stove lid, and then I heard his heavy footsteps trudging back up to the second floor. Was he going for his leather strap (whose persuasive abilities I knew all too well from previous bad decisions I'd made), or was he just heading up to get a new start on his precious few hours of sleep?

Praying he'd make the latter choice, I darted into the kitchen and lifted the stove lid. There was my confiscated library, blue flames licking at its edges. Impulse urged me to plunge my hand right into the stove and salvage what I could, but memory of brother Dan's almost fatal chest burn a few years back kept me from folly. In silent vigil, I watched the pernicious flames melt Plastic Man into Spider Man's web. I watched Bullet Woman, armed with her magic wristbands, vainly trying to fight off the advancing blue-tongued Grim Reaper. The flames turned orange as I watched Batman and Robin and Captain Marvel himself succumb to the collective cremation.

I stood there, humming taps, until only carbon ash remained, and then I respectfully replaced the cast-iron lid. After waiting a suitable interlude to make sure that Pop had gone back to snore land, I crept up the backstairs, avoiding all known creaky steps, and stepped back into my new lair two flights up. Despite the ransacking the room had been through, the taste of freedom was still sweet.

I clicked off the bedside lamp, re-fluffed the pillows, and in the darkness savored the adventure of solitary confinement. Street actions reflected angled light through the room's bay window. The gathering thunder of a trolley car was audible from Madison, grew louder at Crosby, and then peaked in front of our house. The overhead cable line sparked electric juice, energizing the trolley's wobble into town. I heard the Eagle Bar pianist tickling current favorites for the work-weary neighborhood patrons:

"*I'll be seeing you in all the old familiar places that this heart of mine embraces all day through—in that small café, the park across the way, the children's carousels, the chestnut trees, the wishing wells ...*"

"*When the lights go on again all over the world and the boys are home again all over the world, and rain or snow is all that may fall from the sky above ...*"

"*There will be bluebirds over the White Cliffs of Dover, tomorrow just you wait and see.*"

The melancholy crowd crooned along, out of tune but in communion. Drowning their 60-hour week of labor with paychecks from Sun Shipyard, Baldwin Locomotive, Sun Oil, and Baldt Anchor, they downed as many draft brews as their bloodstreams could filter. The poled street lamp cast a spider web image on the ceiling of my new room. Like Spider Man, I climbed each reflected square, inhaling and exhaling contentment beyond song. I then swung through inner space on a thread hung on the skyhook of my imagination.

The measured staccato blasts of the Moyamensing Fire House alarm at Ninth and Potter suddenly startled me back to reality. Its pronouncements echoed through every ward of Chester, rousing to action all volunteers within earshot, whether bellied up to the bar or bedded down like me. This was the big summons, a five-alarmer, so brigades were streaming in from all corners of Chester—Handley Hose, Franklin, Felton, and Goodwill—to lend a hand to the Moyamensing volunteers.

Meanwhile, as the last tune from the Eagle Bar filtered through my putty-blotched window, the regulars departed: ladies exiting through the side entrance on Deshong Street, the men trickling out the front door, exchanging last words for the night. As they dispersed, I dashed to the window in time to listen to the last two stragglers slurring their final dialogue before departure. One leaned on the parking meter; the other propped himself on the pole holding up the streetlight.

As they headed off for separate destinations, the tall one walked as straight as a Marine on guard duty, while the short one with the beer belly zigzagged across the street and disappeared into our side alley.

Historic memory of other drunks and their assaults into our alley alerted me to his intentions. We were prepared for these nocturnal visits, keeping two Bergdoll quart bottles of water on the broad ledge outside our alley window.

149

I went to rouse George, sleeping peacefully in the adjoining room: "George, we've got another live one!"

We rushed to the open window. Just as the relief-seeker was streaming his discharge of processed draft beer on our brick wall, his face turned heavenward in contented relief, George and I working in perfect tandem unloaded both quarts of Chester's prize-winning water on the unsuspecting geezer. Our water bombs dropped their payload into his sighing mouth, drenched his head and shirt, and gravitated southward to his shoes.

The surprise on his countenance as he gulped this tasteless brew started a wheeze in George's throat that bordered on an asthmatic attack. The boozer looked up and caught full view of our faces, hung as they were over the ledge, and gargled a barrage of four-letter zingers never to be found on the approved vocabulary list of Smedley Junior High principal, Margaret Stetser.

He waddled lopsidedly out of the alley, and within seconds our front door commenced to rattle. Although the door was double-bolted, he was making a valiant attempt at home invasion, and George and I were ready for him just in case his outrage gave him enough adrenalin to break through. We held the high ground on the landing outside Mom's bedroom door: I with my Ted Williams-signatured Louisville Slugger, George with an empty Bergdoll milk bottle in each hand.

Soon the door-rattling and the grumbling ceased, and we tiptoed back to the window in time to watch him weave his way up Deshong Street in search of home. We knew our absent brothers would have been proud of our valiant defense of the home front, but we were less sure of Pop's reaction and were grateful that he'd slept through the entire raucous episode.

I followed George up the narrow stairwell to our separate rooms, then returned to my bay-window vantage point to monitor the street action. My pulse throbbed with the syncopated drumbeat of a Woody Herman solo in "Woodchopper's Ball."

A chill of exhilaration contorted my body as I watched the morning trolley turn from Upland, three blocks away, onto Seventh Street. It stopped at Crosby to discharge a hardhat, no doubt a Baldwin Locomotive shift worker. As he disappeared up Crosby Hill, the trolley rolled on toward our house with its one remaining passenger, another weary breadwinner heading home. His head was slumped forward on his chest, bobbing with the ride, and I had a sudden feeling of fear: "Is this your fate, Davey? Are you previewing your life a blink of an eye away?"

Just then a horse-drawn Bergdoll truck clopped into view, stopping directly across the street from our house. Mr. Lynch, our milkman, rattled four quarts as he double-stepped across the cobblestones to our front porch. He planted them on the top step, then hustled back to continue his route. There was a brief delay to respect the needs of his gray-speckled mare, who arched her tail and deposited a load of well-rounded processed oats curbside. Mr. Lynch flicked his reins and rode on down to the Joe Quinn house two doors away.

"Such a neat pile," I thought. "If I can get to it tomorrow morning before anyone else spots it, I'll scoop it and bag it. It should last until Halloween."

My plan was to divide it out in three neat portions, then visit some local notables—porch it, bang on the door, torch the bag, then run like crazy. Mrs. Strayhorn, who worked at the Detention Authority, was at the top of my list. Mr. Collin's porch should also be fertilized. He'd run over the back wheel of my bike with his car and hadn't even apologized. Burt Redden, local politico, was my third candidate, for reasons yet to be explained.

151

I felt like scooping up the steaming pile right then, but I was afraid to disturb Pop. "Let sleeping Pops lie," I was told once by brother Dan, who should know.

A block away, the window-rattling Pennsylvania Railroad express train moved along Chester's elevated track. It was like a tornado gust, harmless unless crossed, and I was resting, wrapped in the shroud of a new dimension of freedom, well out of harm's way.

From my bed, I had a good view of the street lamp outside my window. The mesh was a new addition, put there recently as a sort of vandal barricade by the public works crew, who had also replaced the huge bulb that cast a gargantuan circle of mega-wattage light some 20 feet in diameter. Although I didn't find it quite so offensive from one floor up, that humongous bulb had been a nightly assault on my eight hours of regulation sleep when I'd shared the room below with Pop. If the authorities knew who had taken out the lumens of that original bulb, it would have been reform school for George and me.

One night a few weeks past, we'd climbed out onto the third-floor roof with George's recently acquired Red Rider single-pump BB gun. We'd surveyed the street below, then George had taken aim and with a single shot had cut the city's electric bill. We'd lingered on the roof long enough to catch the pedestrian commentary about the sudden dimming. The inebriates from Millers' Bar were finding it a little more difficult to negotiate the raised quarry-stone curb, and their expletives filled the night.

Burt Redden, party man and chief vote-procurer on Election Day, had been heard to say, "Looks like a local job to me. The neighborhood is unfoldin'." (That astute comment had been enough to put him on my list for the Halloween manure mission).

As he'd sauntered up Deshong to his high-porched house, George and I, mission accomplished, had moved across the tarpapered surface with furtive steps, dropped to the second-floor roof below, reentered the window, wrapped the Red Rider in a towel, buried it in the closet, and bedded down with nary a twinge of conscience.

But Pop had gotten wind of the deed, and despite the long hours he worked to feed his brood, he'd managed to sniff out the culprits. He'd caught George red-handed with the Red Rider and, after failing to break it in half over his muscular thigh, had marched George and his contraband weapon down to the cellar furnace, where he'd unlatched the door and fed the firearm to the flames. As I remembered this tragic event of a few weeks past, I didn't feel quite so bad about Pop's comic-book caper earlier this evening.

As I sat watching the happenings outside my bay window, I thought I recognized someone a block away. He was advancing slowly toward the center of town with a resolute, sober stride, and it looked like our family friend, Mr. Budnick. I made positive identification when the street lamp erased the shadows, and I could clearly see the bucket he carried. It was filled with sponges, chamois, and a 6-foot pole topped with a window squeegee. I watched in respectful silence as he crossed Deshong, negotiated the curb of the Eagles Club, and trudged past Charlie Peck's store. It was a regular ritual for him, no doubt, one that he did during the pre-dawn hours when I usually lay sleeping. It was Mr. Budnick's job to restore clarity to the city's storefront plate glass windows before the business day began, and he did the job to perfection.

Mr. Budnick was a member of our Russian/Ukrainian church at 316 East Eighth Street, and he predictably sat in the right rear section. On Sunday mornings I would always glance across, catch his eye, and see him smile and wink at me, as if he were letting me in on a secret only we would know about.

A few months ago, the *Chester Times* had featured his son Joe's picture in the obituary column: "Killed in action, Anzio Beach, Italy." Come to think of it, I hadn't seen him smile or wink at me since then.

As I watched him walk toward downtown Chester, his head slightly bowed, he seemed to be shouldering the weight of his son's death with each plodding step. But he would still make the windows spotless for the day's shoppers. It was his job.

One floor below I heard Pop stirring. His morning ablutions, the ritual of preparation before departing for work, were beginning. How often I had watched him from my adjacent bed, as George and Paul slept soundly. Pop would drop both feet over the side of the bed, then leaning on right elbow would leverage his strong body to a sitting position, pause as if for inner-ear balance, rub his face from chin to forehead five times, then flat-footedly rise. He'd stand, as if at attention, in jersey and boxer shorts, then he'd walk to the narrow closet, un-hanger his pants, balance on one foot at a time as he slipped them on, pull each suspender up to a shoulder, then walk with tempered movements past Mom's room, take the landing step past Vicky's room, and then five quick steps down the hall to our single bathroom. He'd fill his cupped hands with cold water and use them to splash the water up from face to chin, making a lip-shivering sound I could never reproduce. I was convinced it came from a certain curvature of the lower lip developed by the large number of children sired. Maybe it was futile to try to master it. In fact, I had to towel the floor of splashed water each time I tried to duplicate his efforts.

Pop shaved with bifocals on and raced his Gillette single-edged razor in all directions, using shaving cream

154

whipped to a foam in a thick white cup (of the Boyd diner variety). He'd paint his well-formed face with a shaving brush, usually starting just above the Adam's apple, back-stroking the neck and then swirling the lather across both cheeks from just above the upper lip. He moved with purpose, never prolonging the stare into his own reflected image. He'd save the upper lip until last, stretching it downward over his teeth.

After a few quick rubs to check for stubble, he'd clean the territory—good example to his four sons still at home. He'd walk back to the room, lower his suspender straps, and don a heavily starched white shirt, knot his tie as tight as a hangman's noose, re-shoulder the suspenders, garter his calf-high stockings, grab his closeted coat, and then whisper a loving Ukrainian goodbye into Mom's room.

Then he'd thump his way down the ten rubber-matted steps and take three strides to the front door. The door would open and close gently, and he'd take the three steps down to our cement sidewalk and begin his brisk, purposeful walk to work a block and a half away.

I watched from the bay window three stories up as Pop headed off. Though his sleep had probably been negatively affected by my repeatedly squeaking bed, the caper with the comic books, the drunkard's outrage and his attempted forced entry, Pop was steeled for the upcoming 10-hour day at Roser's Restaurant. His resolute pace picked up speed as he reached Massi's Parking Lot and then Grieco's Print Shop. As Pop turned left at Welsh, he disappeared from sight. Just as Mom began to stir below, dawn gave way to reveal white streaks of cirrus clouds. A cat meowed in the alley (an alto among Mr. Bowen's orchestra of 25 cats), and eddy pools of fall wind stirred up gutter-tossed wrappers.

The window rattled, my eyes blurred with each blink, and my head swirled with the heavy events of my long

155

vigil. It had been my first night alone to will and to do of my good pleasure. I slid off the bed, felt cool linoleum on my knees, heard the distant wail of the freight train whipping through town a block south, and with head in hands and my eyes gathering moisture that substitutes when words seem flimsy, I whispered a prayer:

Help us, Lord, to find our way home. The home you intended for us when our parents heard our first cry, the home parents hoped to make for us by their daily round of sweat and tears. Help the boozer-man seeking relief in our alley to find his way home. Help my brothers come home again to rooms like this. Help the Budnicks look to you for answers to their grief, answers that can come only from you, dear God, keeper of our heavenly home.

I bedded down again, tucked the quilt beneath my chin, and slid the pillow over all but my nose. I breathed in with the full capacity of my lungs and exhaled slowly the breath of my expanding life, as I drifted inward to visions of endless Saturdays.

The Jacket

For a kid who made a career out of being late, I was determined to break the habit on this picture-perfect Friday. I ignored all distractions on my way to Smedley—even the descending gates that halted traffic for the B & O train at Edgmont and Providence avenues. I ran across the tracks as the engineer leaned heavily on the ear-piercing warning whistle, shaking a fist at me as he went by.

I scraped my right arm on the "Stop, Look, and Listen" sign while I glanced backward along the track, sizing up an endless string of boxcars pulled along by the coal-burning engine. As it moved through Chester, the engine spewed a calling card of gray-black smoke —a questionable delight for mothers hanging sheets in the backyard on wash day.

If I hadn't ducked that gate, I'd have been 20 minutes late to school, catching the comments and rolling eyes of Miss Eachus, my homeroom teacher. Instead—thanks to my casual attitude toward the B & O's warning sign—I sauntered to my seat two minutes early.

As I sat looking out the window, I felt at peace with the whole world. Trying to figure out where this calm came from, I suddenly remembered two Saturdays ago when our YMCA basketball team played a league game in Philly. We were losing by two points, with two seconds to go, when I was fouled. I got two foul shots, and I knew if I missed even one of them we were cooked.

This peaceful feeling had cloaked me as I stood at the foul line. I took a deep breath, eyed the rim, shot, and made them both. A good feeling, yes—and for some reason, as I sat staring out the window, it cloaked me again. Was it an omen that something was going to happen today? Well, friend or foe, I'd be ready.

The roll call stopped when the principal clicked the intercom: "Attention! All Smedley Scrappers, report after homeroom to the rear of the school. Today you will be collecting tin cans for the war effort. Please walk to the rear of the school. The truck will be waiting."

The flag salute meant more than ever as I snapped to attention: "I pledge allegiance to the flag of the United States of America and to the Republic for which it stands ..." A side-glance at Betty Schaeffer standing at attention in the next aisle caused more than a patriotic soul-stirring. "... one Nation under God, indivisible, with liberty and justice for all." Al McGrann crouched into the room as the salute ended.

Mr. Joseph piped in again on the intercom, adding a hook to move us pronto: "A group picture of all scrappers will be taken by the *Chester Times* photographer, and the photograph will appear in tomorrow's paper, so come

158

immediately to the rear of the school."

Sure enough, the truck was waiting, so we hopped aboard the rear, leaned on the removable gates, then lined up for a couple of casual shots. Duty done, the driver pulled away with his cargo of proud scrappers aboard. We headed north on Providence Avenue, turned left onto 18th Street, then cruised slowly, stopping wherever bundled cans were stacked.

Reaching Edgmont Avenue, we turned north to cruise slowly past Chester Rural Cemetery on our left and the sacred ground of Saint Michael's Cemetery on the right. As we passed the entry gate of Saint Michael's, a vision of cans appeared—all the cans opened in the lifetimes represented by the rows of grave markers. No more cans to open now. "Will we use can openers in heaven?" my muse whispered.

As our truck turned onto 20th, we sprang into our scrapping action, jumping down to collect the cans that had been placed curbside—flattened, bundled, and stacked. The truck cruised alongside us, two guys remaining on board to grab what we handed them.

Reaching Providence Avenue, the driver turned north, passing Saint Robert's. I spotted a huge bundle at the curb of the McClure mansion and jumped down from the tailgate. In a showoff mood, I hoisted more than I could handle—and tragedy struck. A razor-sharp can lid slit the sleeve of my suede jacket, nicked my shoulder, and drew blood. No need to panic—just a ripped jacket and a scratch. It wasn't enough to abort the trip, so we snaked along all streets this side of Parkside until the truck was full and we returned to school.

Stashing my jacket in my hall locker and grabbing my lunch bag, I headed for the football bleachers to meet the gang. Don Bramble bartered his tomato, lettuce, and pickle sandwich for my peanut butter and jelly. Not

159

exactly an even trade, I thought. Maybe he was just tired of tomatoes.

We chewed away, talking sports between bites, but my thoughts strayed to the ripped jacket hanging in my locker. No way was there enough money to get a new one, and cold weather was just around the corner.

After lunch, I visited the school nurse and showed her my cut, because I was a little worried about lockjaw. She swabbed it with iodine, covered it with a Band-Aid, then scribbled a tardy note for Mr. Ridenour, my woodshop teacher.

My current project, a footstool, was all but finished, but while rubbing on the needed dose of mahogany stain, I swung at a horsefly that landed on the back of my hand and stained my cuff and knuckles instead. When I showed Mr. Ridenour my blunder, he looked at me on an angle, as he was prone to do, with his glass eye staring straight on while his left eye focused on my cuff.

"No charge for the stain, Davey, but your mom will have to give you a pass on the shirt."

Mr. Ridenour understood kids' embarrassments, maybe because of his eye, so when I asked to clean up in the boys' room, he said okay. Even after washing, the stain was engrained in my pores like a smelly tattoo. It was still engrained in the cuff of my shirt, too.

"Nice going, Dave," I thought. "Not only a ripped jacket but a ruined shirt to wear under it." I decided to cut the school day short and head for home.

While walking the hallway to my locker, the bell rang and kids poured out of classrooms like buckshot. And among them was Ann Hughes, walking toward me like an angelic vision. She smiled in passing, so I turned backwards to watch her till she turned the corner. As she turned, she glanced back to see if I was still looking, and

160

she caught me.

It was only last Friday night that I'd walked Ann home from the school dance, and it was on that same night that I wore my ill-fated suede jacket for the first time since George had passed it down to me. I still felt the tingle of our entwined fingers, disentangling before reaching her front porch where her mom sat rocking. Ann was my first walk-home date.

Opening the locker, I stared at the ripped sleeve of my jacket, dangling like an open wound.

"Even if Mom sewed it," I thought, "it would look like a sutured scar on Frankenstein's head."

With inner remorse, I swung the jacket over my shoulder, then headed out for home. Before reaching Deshong Alley, a plan for replacing the star player in my wardrobe was hatched. I slid into our side alley, then into the shed where Mom's Maytag washer stood flanked by the daily pile of dirty clothes.

I knew my shoeshine box was buried somewhere among the unfiled pile of stuff. So I began my frantic search—weeding through two bikes, stacks of old newspapers, galoshes, a flexible flyer, roller skates, toilet plunger, a long-lost yo-yo, an old pair of high-tops, a skate key, two missing war cards, four lead soldiers, an empty bottle of "Evening in Paris"—and finally I reached my shoeshine box lodged in the far corner. Yanking it out, I checked my inventory of polishes, brushes, and rags.

Opening the back door, I spotted Mom and said, "I'm going to walk through town with my shoeshine box, Mom. I'll be home for supper—okay?" She nodded her approval from a hunched position at the ironing board.

Closing the door, I squirmed into my ripped jacket, thinking it might tug at the hearts of payday free-spenders. Knifing down the alleyway, I headed into town.

161

"Got to make some money and get a new jacket before winter sets in," I told myself.

Hurrying up Seventh, I noticed a line of kids outside Saint Michael's Grammar, herded by two nuns who were readying them for their daily walk to Madison Street before dispersing for the day.

Just as the lead nun blew her whistle, signaling the kids to move forward, two men started fighting it out on the crushed cinder parking lot next door. I recognized Yondi Martin's pop, stripped to his jersey, circling a guy I recognized from local barrooms, I never forgot a face that belonged to a hand that tipped me for a newspaper or a shine. Well, his face now trickled blood, and both hands were busy warding off Pop Martin's peppery jabs. This was a sight the nuns felt duty-bound to censor, and they quickly herded their young charges along.

A crowd formed quickly along the lot entrance, bringing Billy Lykens to my side.

"This could be a bloody standoff, Billy. I can't stick around, gotta go, and besides, look who's heading this way."

It was Officer Kandravi, my ticket to reform school. I skirted the combat zone to cut through the alley, emerging onto Welsh Street and starting my mission to replace my jacket.

First stop: the 520 Club. No luck here. The steady churning of the ceiling fans over the long, glossy bar spread tobacco scent to the half-opened swinging door in the grip of my right hand. I waved to Sam Goldberg, the owner, before letting the door swing free. I was on a mission, so I didn't dally.

I double-strutted two blocks to the Chester Arms Hotel, where patrons lounged in overstuffed lobby chairs, faces buried in afternoon editions of the *Philadelphia*

Bulletin and *Chester Times*. Most of them never even acknowledged my inquiry about their scuffed shoes but sat frowning at the printed page like the war had just been lost. On the way out, I picked up a discarded *Chester Times* and browsed through it while walking. The only bad news was that the lousy Yankees beat the St. Louis Cards in the World Series; the good news was that Italy had declared war on Germany.

As I walked along, I wondered how grown-ups could wear so much facial misery, sitting around blowing smoke toward the vaulted ceiling, not even looking me in the face. Not even a "Don't bother me, kid, I'm busy reading."

No sooner had I set up shop a block away than Officer Kandravi gave me a loud warning blast from his whistle. I took this cat and mouse game with the law in stride. It was Kandravi's job to keep streets clear of stragglers, break up fights, chase urchins trying to make a nontaxable buck, maestro midtown traffic, help old ladies across intersections, ticket cars parked a foot away from the curb, and apprehend jaywalkers.

Not wanting a confrontation with the law, I retreated up the steps of the railroad station in search of commuters who valued shined shoes. It was Friday, but this crowd was not in tune with the weekend spirit. I noticed scuffed shoes everywhere, and some men wore pants so short they cuffed out an inch above the ankle— mostly men whose girth forced them to wear their belts above their potbellies.

I soon realized I was wasting my time and headed for the Imperial Arms Café. There wasn't an inch of space at the bar, and a jukebox tune was fighting to be heard over independent dialogues coming from all corners of the room. I decided to try my luck with the booth crowd, glancing pointedly at scuffed shoes as I walked along and trying my best to convey that public opinion hung in the balance. Finally, one of the booth inhabitants hollered out, "Hey, kid, you got cordovan?"

I approached the questioner, slid my right hand into the shoebox, presented cordovan for his inspection, and straddled my box ready to process his request.

Placing his right foot on the template, I launched into action. First the brushing to flick away loose dirt; then a wash with a toothbrush to soften the leather; and then the application of cordovan polish, swirling it into intricately fashioned, symmetrically indented pores of winged tipped leather.

Not a word passed between my customer and me as I practiced my humble profession. He had the dapper look of European nobility, with creases in his pant legs so sharp they could slice a block of Kraft cheese. His drinking buddy had the rough edges of a shipyard foreman and ran all speech through his nose, a perfect Philly accent. They laughed and jabbered while swigging their beer, intent on a long afternoon. Four empties on the table signaled either slow service or fast elbow action.

As I worked, my nose sorted out the smell of pungent Panatelas, lung-coating Camels, and yeasty hops mingling with the collective sweat of the Friday crowd. White and blue collars alike, the work-weary men raised mugs in search of relief from ever-present thoughts of the war.

Just as I was launching into my right-foot finale—a rag-snapping routine I'd learned by watching Sylvester Wilson—I caught a glimpse of green amidst the sawdust under the table. It had the undeniable look of legal tender, and closer inspection revealed it to be a 10-spot.

Thoughts raced faster than my rag snap as I pondered my options. "Do I tell Mister Dapper what resides under his table? Do I lean in, grab the money, then hand it over with a smile, hoping for a tip? Or do I simply accept this as an omen of imminent jacket replacement and try to snag it on the sly?"

I kept on flexing the rag on his right shoe until the answer flashed into my mind faster than Tom Mix chasing a bandito out of town.

I tapped my client's left foot for pedestal position while he and his buddy continued flexing elbows in pursuit of the Examined Life. He positioned his foot without comment, while I prepared for a duplicate effort on his left shoe.

After preliminary brushing, I switched the brush to my left hand, stroked a few passes on the toe, and then let the brush slip like a cannon shot toward the far wall under the booth.

"Doggone it, my brush slipped under the table!" I yelped.

My patron signaled his buddy to open some space for me, and I crawled under, snatched the 10-spot (along with the brush), and inched out. Surreptitiously dropping the crumpled bill into the rear compartment of my box, I embarked on final touches on the propped left shoe, finishing in record time.

"Good shine, kid," my client said with slurred approval, then flipped me a quarter from some spare change sitting in excess suds near his beer coaster.

"Thanks mister," I said, hoisting my box with a casual, streetwise air, as if I was Leo Gorcey playing the lead role in a Dead-End Kids movie. Sauntering to the ladies' exit, I closed the door gently behind me and ran a record 100-yard dash to my side alley.

I entered our lean-to shed, from which I'd emerged a few hours before, and parked my shoeshine box next to the Maytag (after, of course, plucking my bonus 10-spot from the rear compartment and stuffing it deep into my left pants pocket). I took off my ripped jacket and placed it behind the box, thinking it might come in handy the next time I needed to test sentiments of charity.

I eased the kitchen door open, and to my relief Mom was nowhere in sight. I was still feeling jackpot fever over the lucky find under the booth, but doubt was starting to work on my conscience. "When doubt rips the lid from your troubled conscience, pause, reflect, and fix yourself a treat," I told myself.

This adage, paraphrased from my fourth-grade McGuffey Reader, seemed to fit my current situation, so I opened the icebox, grabbed the milk bottle, poured a glass, added two heaping tablespoons of Ovaltine, and stirred it till the granules melted. As I took my first sips, I reasoned thusly:

"How could I be sure the 10-spot belonged to the cordovan guy? If I'd actually seen him drop it and then kept it anyway, I'd reap the whirlwind on Judgment Day for sure. But once before, I'd returned money to someone who swore it was his, and then I'd found out later that he'd lied. If this was a repeat of that betrayal, Mr. Cordovan would have just taken money that wasn't his, soaked up more suds, taxed his overworked kidneys, and quadrupled his stupor. And what if he drove home, then what? If Kandravi nabbed him, it was jail time."

I sat down at the kitchen table, locked in the eternal struggle between right and wrong while slurping the last of my Ovaltine, but my reasonings were definitely tipping my mental scale toward a sense of moral justification.

My struggle ended when a glance at the clock told me that I still had time to run to the Y for a shower, shoot a couple of games of eight ball, scarf down a couple of chili dogs at Jimmy's, and still make it to the Pennsy train station before the *Inquirer* truck pulled in from Philly.

I hollered up the steps to tell Mom my plans, then cut

166

out for my evening paper route.

I made the taproom circuit, barking the war headlines before heading home with $3.22. On the way, I made a brief stop at Ches-Penn Doughnuts and swallowed two glazed in six bites as I walked down Welsh Street. Then, with an added rush of self-indulgence, probably fueled by the 10-spot hiding deep in my left pants pocket, I ducked into Charley Peck's.

With all the firmness my changing voice could muster, I placed my order: "A Pepsi, a box of Cheez-its, five bolsters, five orange slices, and a pint of hand-packed peach for my mom. And please put a little extra on top, because Jim and Paul will come sniffing around for a treat."

Charley gave me an understanding smile and packed my goodies in an extra-heavy brown bag.

Crossing the street, I paused on our sidewalk to salute the five stars in our front window and murmured a silent prayer for the loved ones they represented. I whispered a hurried "amen" when I felt the ice cream melting through the bottom of the bag, then mounted the front steps and pushed the front door open, feeling like a teenage Santa Claus.

Announcing my arrival, I climbed the stairs slowly, wanting to prolong the moment. And sure enough, Jim and Paul were sitting on Mom's bed, wide-eyed with expectation when they saw my bulging bag. I gave Mom the ice cream first, because it was melting, and Paul and Jim got divvies on the candy. I gave them each a swig of Pepsi, then ordered with all the authority of a bigger brother, "Now scram and go brush your teeth. I want to be alone with Mom."

I closed the door of Mom's room, reached into my left pocket for the $10 bill, then into my right pocket to snag the four quarters remaining from my paper route—

placing it all into Mom's upturned palm. To see her expression was worth all the gold in Fort Knox.

As I kissed her left temple, she whispered, "Davey, I want you to have this money to buy something you really want, something special that you pick out, something not passed down from your older brothers."

I sat beside Mom for a while, thinking about her offer. As my eyes started to cloud, I noticed that hers were clouding, too.

"Something special, something YOU like," she said, then closed her eyes and became lost in reverie.

Sensing this, I asked, "Mom, did you ever get anything special, something you liked, something that was yours from the start?"

She looked at me as if I'd read her mind. Her left hand moved to her earlobe, pinching it between her thumb and forefinger, and then she said, "Yes, Davey, I did once have something special. When I boarded the ship for America, I couldn't read, write, or speak a word of English, so they pinned my name and destination on my coat and placed me in what they called steerage."

"Is that the name for the bottom part of the boat, where they put all the poor people?" I asked her, thinking back to some of my history lessons at Smedley.

Mom nodded. "To me it seemed like the Jonah story my mother used to read to me from the Bible. It seemed like I sat in the bowels of that ship for eternity, everyone around me sick and heaving. I almost gave up hope of ever getting out of that hole, but we made it. All I had in this world was what my mom packed into my trunk ... and one other special gift that I wore. When I left for America, she knew we would never see each other again until we met in Heaven, so close to the day I was to go, she pierced my ears. And when they healed, she placed golden earrings in my lobes."

My mom's sweet face beamed in remembrance. "My words fail me, Davey, when I try to share how I felt, looking into the mirror with my mother smiling over my shoulder. I've carried the memory of her smile and her gift of my golden earrings in my heart ever since."

"What happened to your earrings, Mom?" I asked. "I never saw you wear them."

Mom heaved a long sigh, then said, "When I arrived in Philadelphia to live with my brother John, I was given a job at a clinic. Well, when I was at work one hot summer day, I removed my earrings to wash and freshen up. While drying my face in a towel, I turned my back on where I placed them, and when I turned around again, they were gone. My golden earrings, my most special treasure, vanished—just like that."

Mom snapped her fingers to show how quickly the awful event had happened.

A lump had formed in my throat as Mom shared her story in her soft-spoken way. I kissed her, then hugged her tight around the neck. This was the only answer I could give to her shared memory. As I left her side, she slipped the $10 bill back into my hand.

I walked the hallway to the bathroom, brushed my teeth, then climbed the stairs to my new third-floor room, where I sipped Pepsi, crunched Cheez-its, and read Captain Marvel comic books to the symphonic backdrop of trolley wheels and rusted-out mufflers down on the street. When the Eagle Bar ushered its last patrons out at two in the morning, I slowly sank into sleep, wondering who now wore Mom's golden earrings.

I awoke at nine, the jarring sound of the alarm clock yanking me out of my dreams. After morning ablutions, I fixed my Saturday special, a bowl of Wheaties buried beneath a thinly sliced banana and milked to the brim, followed up with a pack of Tastykakes.

It was nine thirty when I left for town, my 10-spot back in my right pants pocket. "Get something special," Mom had said. And for me it was a jacket.

Random thoughts surfaced as I walked into town. I started to grapple with the who and why questions that plagued me once in a while. Why wasn't I born first so I could be in the war and brother Mickey could be walking down the streets of Chester on this October morning? Why weren't we rich so we could live above the B & O tracks and have a front porch and grassy lawn? Why didn't somebody ram a bayonet in Hitler's gut and end this rotten war?

My brother John once told me we were so poor we weren't allowed to window shop. I thought it was just a comment on reality but found out later he'd told me an old Henny Youngman joke. "Well, today, John, I'm going to do more than window shop," I said. "I'm going to buy."

I hit Speare Brothers first. A clerk appeared out of nowhere, almost as if he was waiting for me, but I told him I just wanted to look around. He nodded and walked away but kept me in his peripheral vision while I fingered my way through the racks along the wall.

"If I were a clerk, I'd keep an eye on a kid in my shabby condition, too," I admitted to myself. When I walked out a few minutes later, my backward glance caught the relief on his face.

I spent about five minutes watching the window dresser rearrange the mannequins in Murray's but didn't go in, pretty sure I'd get the same reception I'd just gotten in Speare's. I decided to walk down Market to Fourth, where I'd try my luck at Canter's Army and Navy Store.

There I tried on a Navy pea coat, but after checking

170

myself in the mirror I decided I'd wait for John to come home from the war. Maybe he'd give me his. I left Canter's in an upbeat mood, feeling like I knew how to get around town, how to take short-cuts through all the alleys, how to sense trouble coming and somehow get away, how to size people up or down, and which dogs to pet and which to leave alone.

I loved this city with all its meandering streets and patchwork neighborhoods, each with its dominant culture but also a healthy sprinkling of other minorities, all living together in peace. Chester was a giant hoagie with hot and sweet peppers loaded with provolone, prosciutto, ham, pickles, onions, salami, tomatoes, lettuce, oregano, and oil, all stuffed in a roll as fresh and long as a summer day. My emotional taste buds salivated to taste it all.

I looked down Third Street to the bridge crossing Chester Creek and mentally traced my footsteps all the way to Saint Anthony's Church, where families could worship and pray for sons and daughters fighting in a war to regain freedom for the very towns their parents left to come to America. And beyond, further down the street, the Polish worshipped at Saint Hedwig's and prayed for families left to suffer the dregs of war in a country overrun by Hitler and his henchmen. Saint Hedwig's was where we crashed wedding receptions for love of food with names we couldn't pronounce.

I turned to watch the trolley roll onto the turnaround in the Market Square. The people stepped off, and the conductor pushed it around on its circular dish, ready to roll all the way back from whence it came: 69th Street. I followed it as I walked up Market Street until it took its dog-leg turn under the Sixth Street underpass.

My next target in quest of a jacket was Sears Roebuck, but when I saw Dudley Wilson heading my way, I crossed the street in a hurry. I knew if he spotted me

171

he'd want to come with me, and the last thing I needed was a distraction from finding a new jacket. So I crossed the street in a hurry, ducked into the alcove of Spencer's Stationery and browsed the display window until Dudley walked beyond A. S. Beck Shoe Store.

Sears Roebuck was couched hard against the railroad station. Entering with high expectations, I soon found that it might be a great place to buy tools but their jacket selection was out to lunch.

Next stop was Adam's Clothes. Continuing up Edgmont Avenue, I came to a sudden stop at the Quaker Graveyard. I rubbed my eyes in disbelief as I watched gravediggers lift Chester's earliest settlers out of grave sites. Wasn't a grave a hallowed place not to be tampered with? I watched as a casket, maybe 300 years old, was placed beside the heap of earth that had covered it.

I hoisted myself to a better position to watch this sacrilege. Caskets lay everywhere, all sizes. Some of them held the bones of William Penn's buddies, Quaker shipmates who came with him on *The Welcome*. They planned the layout of streets, built the courthouse on Market Street, served as judges on Pennsylvania's first Supreme Court. Now their caskets lay in the sun where stray dogs could lift a leg on their dishonored remains.

"Desecration!" my mind shouted. "Someday this city will suffer for this decision."

As I dropped from my perch, I overheard a passerby tell a friend, "The city decided to move the graveyard to make room for a new department store. All in the name of progress, I guess."

Walking toward Seventh Street, Pop's oft-repeated biblical quote raced through my thoughts: "Teach us, Lord, to number our days and apply our hearts unto wisdom." This grave-robbing move today, I thought, was not a wise decision.

172

Entering Adams Clothes, I walked through the store, convinced I'd know what I liked when I saw it. But I found nothing on the racks to excite my interest.

My last planned stop was Montgomery Wards, a block away. It was a perfect day. The sun slanted its rays through low clouds, and a crisp breeze swirled pockets of leaves on the fenced lawn of Saint Michael's Church Rectory. I stopped to look at the jewelry and watches in Doubet's display window and said hello to Mr. Gayley as he stood rearranging the rake display in front of his hardware store.

Entering "Monkey Wards," I looked around, but again it was to no avail. I stood outside the store, uncertain what to do next. Maybe sit on the Y steps and watch Saturday shoppers walk through town? Maybe walk over to Deshong Park and see who's playing ball? Maybe just give up and head toward home? I cut through Saint Michael's Rectory, then vaulted the iron fence into the yard next to Charlie Peck's store, where I stepped inside for a treat for my sagging spirit.

"A Royal Crown and a pack of Crumpets will do it for now, Mr. Peck," I called out. He looked a little surprised when I handed him a 10-spot, but he gave me my change without comment.

I sat in the booth near the pinball machine, listening to the pings and racket created by a master of timing, meaningful finger, and palm motion. It was none other than Buster Robinson, racking up more free games than he could play in the next six hours.

I left Charlie's with no expectation of finding what I wanted today, so I decided to head toward Tucker's Pool Room before going home in jacketless defeat. (Pop had declared Tucker's off-limits, but good old Tucker wore glasses so thick he couldn't tell how old I was, and besides I just stood around and watched the action.)

As I headed toward Tucker's, I passed John's Small Profit Store and noticed a jacket sleeve partially buried under other clothing in the display window. I entered the store, catching the owner leaning into his lunch—a can of beans sitting on a hot plate fueled by a can of Sterno.

"Cheap John" was a man of few words and allowed browsers all the freedom needed to roam and rummage. He knew me by sight. I'd lived right across the street for six years, and in all that time he'd never once caught me soaping his store windows on Halloween. I couldn't prove it, but I'd bet a pack of Wrigley's gum that John's inventory was mysteriously transferred from the Chester Rescue Mission, or else he sent runners to tap the Salvation Army drop boxes.

The huge room was pungent with the odor of mothballs. Peeling paint flaked on all visible walls, rust stains announced pipe leaks somewhere beyond the tin corrugated ceiling, and the dirty display windows hadn't been scrubbed in years. Cheap John was well named. He had little competition and kept a low overhead.

John's cash register was his left front pocket—I noticed the bulge. After lifting the jacket from the pile in the display window, I tried it on. Checking my image in the cracked mirror near the back of the store, I realized it fit like a glove.

It was gray wool with slanted pockets. I bent my elbows to check the flex—ah, enough freedom for extended jabs in an unprovoked fight. I ran my palms down the smooth front, slid my fingers into pockets deep enough to swallow my wrists, roomy enough to make a clenched fist.

I worked the zipper from bottom to top a couple of times, checking for snags. The zipper handle was engraved with a single word: "TALON." It was a heavy-duty zipper with a musical sound.

I stood, admiring my reflection. A side glance caught Cheap John still hunched over his Sterno. He seemed intent on getting to the bottom of his tin can before turning attention to a potential sale. He had the appearance of a bark-stripped tree with withered branches, and I guessed that he was pretty old.

"How many more cans of beans will John scarf down," I wondered, "before his gravestone is positioned in Saint Michaels Cemetery?" (This I surmised from a picture of the Virgin Mary hanging on the wall.)

Looking into the cracked mirror, feeling my pulse rise like healthy sap, I knew I had picked a prize. But what about Cheap John? He wasn't long for this world, and I felt there was nothing I could do about it but barter my way into this trophy from his inventory and add a little cash to the bulge in his pocket.

Grateful for my youth and the long road ahead of me, I closed my eyes and envisioned the scene repeated in Chester every Sunday morning—cadets from the Pennsylvania Military College marching in rank down Madison Street to the Episcopal church on Ninth. They moved in perfect cadence, sporting jackets like the one I was about to bargain for. I imagined myself marching with them, not missing a parade-dress movement. I heard an observer calling out, "Who is that lad bringing up the rear? He looks like one of the Komarnickis."

"How's it fit, kid?" Cheap John suddenly asked around a mouthful of beans. "How's it fit?" he repeated, snapping me from reverie to a bartering world.

"Okay, I guess—a little tight. Maybe it'll fit my kid brother better."

He turned towards me, retorting offhandedly, "Looks okay from here, let you have it for nine bucks."

"Nine bucks!" I countered. "Are you kidding me?

175

That's three days' work in a sweatshop—no way!" (Boy, did I want that jacket.)

John turned, still swallowing beans, watching while I took the jacket off and laid it down. I dug into randomly stacked piles on tables and walked around looking disinterested. I knew the routine of the barter. I'd learned it from brother Dan when he took me to Krass Brothers on South Street in Philly, where we walked out and were halfway down the block before Krass himself whistled us back.

"Patience, Davey," I told myself. "Feign disinterest; walk out if that's what it takes." I started heading toward the front door.

When John sensed I was about to leave the premises, he grunted, "Okay, okay, since you're a neighbor, it's yours for seven bucks."

I walked toward him and looked him straight in the left eye. (My brother John had once told me the left eye is the most vulnerable to suggestion.)

"With all due respect, Mister, I'd like to buy in the neighborhood, but seven bucks for a tight jacket is like fleecing a lamb, and I'm no lamb. Look, I got to go sell newspapers, so I can't stay and bicker. So it's four bucks, or I'm out the door."

I stared him down for three seconds while he swallowed the beans and the offer. I turned to go, and just as my Joe Lapchick sneaker hit the threshold, Cheap John bellowed, "For you, kid, it's a deal."

I did an immediate about-face into the store and fingered four singles from my pocket. I mentally congratulated myself for stopping at Charlie Peck's on the way, so I wouldn't have to hand him the 10-spot and show him how prosperous I really was.

As I turned to leave, my folded gray jacket with the

176

slanted pockets cradled in my arms, John said "Where'd you learn to barter, kid? You're good."

I knew he was pumping me up, trying to make me feel like I'd maneuvered a deal, so I tried to pump him up too. "You won't regret this," I said from the doorway. "I've got plenty of friends, and when they see me sporting this jacket, they'll be asking where I got it."

Well, if Cheap John did snatch his inventory from the Salvation Army, he just made a whopping profit of four bucks. But I wasn't about to question the source from whence my good fortune came. I accepted it as a gift, and as brother George once told me, "Never look a gift horse in the mouth, Dave. It might bite."

So I wore my gift home, leap-straddled a parking meter while waiting for the trolley to pass, then 10 giant steps across the street, and I was in the house. I hurried to the kitchen, where Mom turned from domestic preparations to give me all the audience a kid needed. She stood with her left hand on her hip, right hand extended to her cheek, and with a smile she radiated her admiration.

"Turn around," she said.

This I did, reveling in her approval.

"Perfect fit, Davey. You look so handsome."

While turning, I almost reached into my pocket to hand over the change from the 10-spot and boast about my bargain. But I kept quiet. If I gave her the money now, she'd just spend it on feeding her brood. I had other ideas.

Mom sat me down at the kitchen table, where she sliced two potatoes, scooped them into the mesh basket of the french fryer, and lowered them into the already bubbling grease.

When the fries were ready, she lifted a huge bowl

from the cupboard and poured the fries into it. Then we bowed our heads while Mom gave thanks. Her words carried a lilting Ukrainian accent as she uttered them in her adopted English language, pleading God's protection of her sons and an end of the war.

We lingered at the kitchen table, sharing the bowl of french fries, celebrating my first big purchase—a serendipitous gift resulting from the sighting of a piece of green on a barroom floor.

Finally the long day's journeys caught up with me, and I kissed Mom goodnight and headed up to my third-floor room. There I dug my White Owl cigar box out of my closet, pulled five crumpled dollar bills from my right pants pocket (I kept the coins), and carefully stashed them under the other treasures I kept there. It wasn't enough yet, but maybe someday I could give Mom back that special feeling of wearing something brand-new, something bought just for her. Maybe someday her lobes would again be sporting golden earrings, bought by a grateful son who'd stashed his cash toward that joyful, "something special" day.

P.S. Other jackets have since draped my frame. George handed down a multi-colored sports jacket, which gave me peer-group stature. And after the war, I paraded downtown Chester in John's U.S. Navy pea coat and felt the vicarious thrill of commanding a torpedo boat. When I donned Joe's Army Air Force leather jacket, I felt like Dana Andrews in "The Best Years of Our Lives."

But memory of that jacket bartered from Cheap John conjures feelings that rarely come along. I've been waiting for another visit of that euphoric feeling ever since.

Ash Wednesday

I felt like a month of Saturdays as I hit the sidewalk running to catch the bus to Chester High. Ordinarily I'd walk, but I'd overslept—and now that I was 15, I was trying to break the late habit. My roster of tardies at my alma mater, Smedley Junior High, had been so lengthy that my homeroom teacher, Miss Eachus, had declared me the school record-holder, based upon the hard evidence of her 20 years of roll-calling experience.

Reaching the bus stop, I leaned against the YMCA wall and waited, hoping to spot a friend with wheels. Instead my eye caught Buster Robinson standing across the street, straight-arming a pole and waiting for the light to turn green. This uncharacteristic adherence to traffic etiquette stemmed solely from the presence of Officer Kandravi, who could shatter an eardrum with his lip-clenched whistle if moves were made to cross on the red.

Buster, who possessed a face and frame along the lines of Gary Cooper, was two years my senior and a major force in the enlarging circle of my life. It was he who had mentored me in the craft of shooting marbles, teaching me how to knuckle down and how to use a steelie to power-drive marbles out of the ring. In time I'd gotten so good I welcomed all comers anytime, anywhere.

One day Buster brought me a brown cotton work glove, cut off at the fingers, and gave it to me so I could practice all winter on frozen ground. Soon I was wiping out all the neighborhood kids. I bested them all: Doodles, Ernie Gatta, Harvey, Sylvester Wilson, Sonny Lynch, Dudley, Paul Lukes. In fact, I busted everybody but Buster. After each game, I'd offer the marbles back for cash, 30 for a nickel.

I was still leaning against the Y wall when the light changed and Buster crossed.

"What's up, Davey?" he asked.

"I'm waiting for the bus. Don't want to be late for school," I told him.

"You'll never make it," he said. "Next bus gets you there 10 minutes past bell-time. I should know after three years." Buster paused, looked down, then said casually, "I'm thinking of catching Louie Armstrong at the Earle Theatre in Philly. Forget school, Davey. Come with me."

As I considered his proposition, my mind flashed back to a similar offer he'd made six years before.

*　　*　　*

I was nine years old, sitting on the granite step in front of my house. Eleven-year-old Buster waved me across the street and laid out a temptation I couldn't resist: "Davey, the State Theater has its grand opening today. Want to go with me?" Then he added the final lure

180

that got the best of my vulnerable conscience: "I'll pay."

I got so excited I accepted the offer without asking Mom if I could go. Pop placed movies just below street fights in the hierarchy of time-wasters, and I wasn't going to risk getting my first theater outing nixed before it started. Buster and I walked together up Seventh to the State and took our place in a line snaking past the State House Restaurant, Henry's Clothing Store, and into the alley past the entrance to Royal Billiards.

Finally we entered the lobby, and I inhaled a coolness of air I'd never felt before. We stormed the carpeted stairs to the balcony, where we were greeted by an usher decked out in an outfit I wouldn't wear on a dare. He led us to seats smack up against the projection room wall, where I sat squirming with quiet excitement.

When the projector flashed the first spectrum of overhead light, a new world unfolded before my eyes. After the first feature came to a satisfying crime-doesn't-pay conclusion, Buster leaned over to me, whispering, "I got to go, Davey. See you later."

I nodded and stayed on, mesmerized, until two shows later— clueless that five hours had passed. The sky was dark when I finally walked out, and it wasn't until I checked the clock at Smith's Newsstand that I realized it was 8:10. I flew home in a gulping panic, belatedly realizing my folly.

Sneaking into the house by way of the kitchen, I discovered Mom crying. Overjoyed to see me, she rose to her feet and hugged me with all the strength love could muster, then sat again, drying her eyes on her flour-encrusted apron.

Only then did Mom unfold the seriousness of my plight. When Pop had come home and learned I hadn't showed for supper, deep and abiding worry had struck him. He'd thought maybe the gypsy wagon had kidnapped me and spirited me away to Bohemia. So he'd hustled four blocks to the police station and waited till they dispatched a squad car to search for me. Then Pop had gotten restless and decided to speed the search by checking the streets and alleys himself.

When Mom revealed all this to me, I realized that not only had I missed my supper but I'd also missed serving my evening paper route, a loss that would put a crimp in my lunch money for the week. All that and the anticipated agony of Pop's strap created dry heaves, so I ran upstairs to hide, thinking maybe he'd grow tired and go to bed before he found me.

When Pop finally came home from his fruitless searching, Mom relieved his worry by telling him I was safely in the house. He finally spotted me under Mom's bed, lodged in the far corner near the wall, hidden by an old army blanket. A sneaker I'd failed to cover was my undoing, and he yanked me out by my leg. Then in very measured tones he asked me to account for my whereabouts. Knowing how he'd respond to the truth, I beat around the bush until the strap came out and it was my hind parts that got beaten.

*　　　*　　　*

It was this not-so-tender memory that I was focusing on when Buster raised the issue of hookying school for another illicit theater outing. Six years hadn't dimmed the recall of Pop's well-placed strap.

"I couldn't go if I wanted to, Buster," I stalled. "I've only got a half-a-buck, and besides Mr. Wren is hitting us with a math test today."

While Buster rifled his pockets for the necessary coin inventory to stake me, a guy standing within earshot piped up with a side-mouthed comment, "Hey, kid, do you really want to hooky school?"

I turned and studied the stranger's face. He looked like a weathered sailor who had showered in cold salt water for four years. He was waiting for an answer. Meeting his gaze, I said, "Yeah, I do. I really do."

"Okay, follow me."

I left my wall-leaning position immediately, and Buster and I followed two paces behind the stranger, crossing Edgmont Avenue to Smith's Newsstand, where he barked, "A pack of Chesterfields, a *Chester Times,* and give me the change in ones."

He handed Smitty a $20 bill, and the order was filled pronto. Then the weather-beaten Daddy Warbucks clamped the *Chester Times* under his left arm, tapped out a cigarette, lit it with his stainless-steel Ronson, then inhaled with such lung-collapsing force that the nicotine must have been vacuumed down to his toes. With smoke streaming out both nostrils, he spread the singles out at my eye level. They looked like a George Washington fan.

"How many do you need, kid?"

I looked at Buster, then back to the bucks— contemplating my golden moment. Then my inner voice whispered four words from the archive of Pop's Ponderables, words grooved in memory while the turkey platter reached me in mid-passage around the Thanksgiving table. Pop, in his throat-clearing, Ukrainian-vintage baritone, had cautioned, "Don't be hog, Davey."

Now, as I stood gawking, I took Pop's recollected pronouncement as an omen and stifled my greed impulse. I slowly tweaked four crisp dollar bills from the handheld offering, taking them one by one and in the process letting him know that his gift would be remembered. He tapped me on the head with his folded paper and grinned. "Enjoy it, kid, you only live once. And after all life's one big hooky, ain't it?"

183

As I watched my benefactor cross Welsh Street, I wondered if his generosity had anything to do with the fact that the war in Europe had just ended and he was grateful to have made it home. I silently vowed that someday some other kid would feel the thrill I was feeling right then.

Buster checked his wristwatch, then said, "The Philly local leaves at 8:10. We can make it if we move it, so let's go."

We hustled down Edgmont to the Pennsy Railroad station, turning at Sixth to cut through the underpass. Buster bought tickets and sent me off to dump my telltale school books in a rentable locker. It was like having a street-wise older brother who handled the details.

We sprinted up the first flight of steps two by two, then paused at the first landing and took the others like seasoned commuters. The morning crowd didn't give us a second glance. Some had their faces buried in newspapers, others paced the white marble floor as if late for an appointment, and some of the more laid-back types relaxed along a contoured mahogany bench that ran the length of the room.

We walked out onto the wide, wood-planked northbound platform, anxious to be among the first to spring aboard. This was my first Philly trip without one of my real-life big brothers, and those pre-war memories were sparse and shadowy. In a peripheral eye scan of the territory, I noticed the railroad detective leaning on the wall near the concession stand, turning pages of a *Public Ledger* while he surreptitiously read the crowd. If I'd been alone I'd have had a tough time explaining my solo trip to the Big City, but somehow my association with Buster gave me credibility.

The train coasted in, the conductor swung down and bellowed "All aboard!", and commuters moved forward like tilted sand in an upturned hourglass. Mounting the steel steps, I entered a half-filled car and plopped into an empty seat next to the window while Buster slid into one across the aisle. The clips on my window were jammed. and I didn't have any luck unjamming them, so I had to listen to the repetitious rhythm of steel on steel through the open window as we moved along the track toward Philadelphia 's Suburban Station.

I sat in awed silence, stashing away the sights like a kid who's been told he's about to go blind. Glancing across the aisle, I caught Buster's profile framed by the window and wished I could read his thoughts and know why he'd adopted me—of all the kids in the neighborhood. When I turned back to look through my own window, I saw that the train was crossing over the Ridley Creek trestle, and—WHAMMO—I was hit with as clear a memory as ever paid me a visit.

*   *   *

I was 11. A gang of us were playing on the B & O railroad tracks high above Chester Creek when Paul Lukes dared me to cross the trestle. Crossing first, he egged me on to follow. I edged my way halfway across, then looked down between the railroad ties to the churning water below. My legs locked, and I stood motionless—frozen with paralyzing vertigo, as far off in the distance I heard the shrill warning of an advancing train.

"If I make a move and my foot slips between the rails," I thought, "it will be Doomsville for me." Fear rose like a tidal wave as terminal thoughts took over: "Is this all there is for you, Davey? If only Mickey or John or Joe or Dan were here to get me out of this mess, I'll never play on the tracks again. LORD, HELP ME!"

I turned my head to check how much time I had

185

before I met my maker, and instead I saw Buster stepping lively toward the middle of the tracks. When he finally reached me, he put his hands out, palms up, and said, "Easy, Davey. Don't panic."

Hoisting me piggyback, he sprinted across the trestle, touching down nimbly on each spaced railroad tie, then dropped me on the embankment seconds before the freight train screeched by with its ominous death wail. I lay on my belly, stunned and shivering, watching as the boxcars rolled on and on.

*   *   *

"Next stop Lansdowne; Lansdowne next station stop," the conductor called out. I settled back against the seat and for the next 10 minutes enjoyed the sights rolling by the open window, conscious that today's adventure was an extension of the gift Buster had given me when he'd plucked me from certain death four years ago. This ride was life to the fullest—rolling into Philly on my first high school hooky, with Louie Armstrong and his trumpet waiting in the wings.

As the train reached Philadelphia, it tunneled like a steel-encased mole through dimly lit archways, finally surfacing onto elevated tracks that took us toward the heart of town. From this vantage point I had a good view of what Mr. Jolley, my history teacher, called the "cradle of civilization." The train suddenly submerged again and eased silently into Suburban Station.

After detraining, I followed Buster as he hustled through the impressive 1920s-vintage station. Most of the underground shops were still closed, dimly lit and fronted with meshed steel gates.

We finally reached a door that opened to an outside stairwell. Opening the door, we were greeted with a near knockout blow to the nose. The steps were impregnated with urine sprayed on them by a legion of bladder-loaded

186

unfortunates who apparently sought regular relief on this particular stairway. I was no stranger myself to nocturnal emergencies, and I remembered wetting the bed one subzero winter night when my only other option had been a trip to the outhouse in our backyard.

The weather was brisk and breezy when Buster and I emerged into the sunlight, and a steady stream of traffic was circling the island of City Hall that straddled Broad and Market. I paused for a minute to gawk at the statue of William Penn perched atop this hive of city government. A cloudless blue sky formed a backdrop for Mr. Penn, who was looking down with benediction upon all who passed below. Buster stood with his hands in his pocket, indulging my sense of wonder. No need to hurry. We had two hours till curtain time.

Slanting across Market Street, we detoured through the walkway that cut through City Hall. In an arched alcove in the center courtyard, I spotted a sailor pinning his girl flush against the granite wall in a passionate embrace. "That's what won the war," I mused to myself. "Passion and lots of ammunition."

I wondered if brother Mickey had planted a kiss like that on his girl, Myra, when he returned from the service. And what about brother John? He'd do it without batting an eye. John never sweated public opinion.

As we exited the courtyard onto Market East, I looked up to the second-floor windows across the street and noticed a window washer strapped in space, executing his strokes like a true pro, no wasted motion. Above his extended squeegee, a major sign was draped. It extended across two windows and announced, "ALLINGER'S BILLIARD ACADEMY—MOSCONI VS. PONZI—1 P.M. TODAY." I paused, pointed, and Buster agreed. We'd have time to catch it, since our train back to Chester wasn't pulling out until 4:02. I couldn't believe it. Mosconi, the greatest pool player in the universe, and we were going to see him play. But first we had an appointment with Satchmo.

I felt alive to the street life of Philadelphia. Pop had met Mom here, and they'd gotten married in Saint Mary's Church just a couple of miles away. My sister Mary had been born on Delancey Street. Then they'd moved to American Street, and on boiling hot nights she and brother Mickey would sleep on the sidewalk in front of the house. I wondered why Pop had decided to move to Chester. I'd have to ask him sometime, but not on a hooky day.

Walking east on Market, I cataloged everything that moved, almost as if I were a country boy making my first trip to the big city. A peanut vendor, temporarily ignoring his customer, was ogling a thin-ankled beauty as she crossed the street. I couldn't fault him, having occasionally focused on a shapely leg as I eased a dainty foot into a patent-leather pump while working at A. S. Beck Shoe Store back in Chester.

My eyes shifted to a pretzel hawker. He sported an ear-flapped hat buttoned beneath a receding chin, an ancient leather jacket, baggy pants, unlaced combat boots, and a cigarette dangling from his mouth. Just then a soldier strode by, causing the pretzel hawker to stop in the middle of his pitch. He seemed frozen in thought, as if the sight of the Army uniform conjured up battle scenes from World War I, perhaps snapshot memories of himself surviving a mustard gas attack by German troops. It seemed ironic that now he was standing on a Philadelphia street, huckstering mustard-spread pretzels to a bustling crowd.

A girl walking five paces ahead of us caught my eye, as she tried to restrain a bulldog on a leash. Her jet-black hair reached to her waist, and it was dancing in the wind. She wore Levi's, cut above the knees, and moved with a ballerina's grace. I doubled my stride to catch a glimpse of her face, curious to see if it matched up to the rest of her. Just then two ancient nuns, approaching life's final curtain, looked my way. They smiled knowingly at me, seeming to read my thoughts.

The light flicked green, and a married couple crossed 13th Street with their children, the mother with a viselike grip on her daughter's hand and Dad holding the toes of a younger version of himself sitting astride his shoulders.

We arrived at the theater in time to watch a line form behind us and ultimately wind around the corner. It was 9:45 when we reached the ticket window. Minutes later we stepped onto the plush red carpet, then headed down the long, sloping aisle toward empty seats waiting for us in the second row. Perfect, perfect, perfect—full view of the stage. I looked around—this was obviously no popcorn crowd, and I wouldn't be finding any gum planted under the seats.

"That stage is wider than my house and Sonny Lynch's next door put together," I observed to Buster.

The lights dimmed, the stage curtains parted, and the brass blasted the packed house. I was reeled in like a hooked fish when Louie walked on and stood center stage, flashing his full-face grin. With a loose handkerchief dangling from his trumpet hand, he began tapping his foot to the syncopated rhythm, getting ready to swing his horn from hip to lip and orchestrate the roller coaster rhythm we'd all come to ride. The band opened on an upbeat rendition of "Mack the Knife," and Louie leaned into the microphone, graveling the lyric with effortless ease.

From my second-row vantage point, I could feel the heat of the overhead stage lights and see the sweat beads already rippling down Louie's brow as he glided into his second number, his own version of "One O'Clock Jump."

189

His eyes bulged and sparkled with the flush of creative joy as he worked his horn. I saw him scanning the crowd for eye contact, and then suddenly I felt his eyes catch mine and I was pulled totally under Satchmo's spell. Without pause he segued into "Ain't misbehavin'/I'm savin' my love for you," which relaxed the crowd from the forward lean they'd assumed during the last number.

I'd read about Louie in a fan magazine. At 45 he was exactly three times as old as I was. He'd had 30 more years of living, and he'd filled them with endless cycles of improvised jazz. As he ran up the scale to a neck-bulging octave that would arouse dog howls if we were outside, Louie seemed to go off into a detached reverie. I let my mind take off, too, thinking about some of the similarities in our lives.

From what I'd read, he'd started out pretty much the same as me—dirt-poor but inventive. At age 12 our similarities had converged but had different results. He'd fired a gun at a New Year's celebration and had been rewarded with two years of reform school. I'd helped my brother George shoot out a streetlight with a Red Rider BB gun and had gone to bed.

Louie's two-year stint in reform school gave him the opportunity to learn the cornet, and then he was released at 14 to pursue fame. At the same age, I'd had free lessons on the cornet at the Salvation Army, but my romance with a mouthpiece had ended when I'd split my lip wide-open with a homemade rubber-gun. I guess there was a moral in there somewhere if I wanted to dig for it, but right now I was digging the orchestra's rendition of "Jeepers Creepers."

The sentimental journey meandered on to "I'm gonna buy a paper doll that I can call my own," and when that was finished Louie paused to hit the spittle-release button, wiping his trumpet clean with his dangling handkerchief. He then hypnotized the crowd with "Up the Lazy River." Like a lot of true stars, Louie seemed to take delight in sharing the spotlight with his orchestra. He turned after each number to acknowledge them, and as the numbers unfolded he featured each instrument in solo: saxophones, piano, drums, bass, and even the other trumpets.

Then the orchestra floated the crowd away with a final exclamation mark—launching into "Grab your coat and get your hat/Leave your worries on the doorstep/Life can be so sweet/On the sunny side of the street."

On that high note the curtain descended. The audience responded with ear-splitting whistles and raucous catcalls for an encore, but the curtain stayed down. Louie was spent, and in truth I was pretty drained myself. It was an awakening for a 15-year-old kid from Chester. If life was a hooky, as my personal Daddy Warbucks had said, then this hooky was my introduction to life. Today I'd moved into awareness of a dimensional universe I'd yet to explore, and sound and rhythm were leading the way.

I sat for a while, reflecting on the carnival feeling of the day as the crowd inched up the aisle. Buster, always a lead dog, tapped my arm and said, "Let's go. I've got a surprise for you."

Once outside, he picked up the pace as we walked back towards City Hall. We wove an inside-outside pattern across cobblestone streets, scanning buildings, packed trolleys, trucks spewing diesel fuel into the face of a mounted policeman, cabs moving at the speed of tips, and—all along the way—people.

There were Italians arguing with elaborate hand motions, shoppers checking out the window displays, and street hucksters trying to steer people into their stores. There were knicker-clad kids, old geezers getting their mile workouts, and a man skinny as a flute walking alongside a woman the size of a bass fiddle.

There was a dapper gent wearing spats and holding on to old times. There was another, no doubt in the grip of hard times, wearing a sandwich board that announced the best beef and ale in town. A midget walked along the curb, seeming wary that someone might fall on him. A strutter practiced his moves for the New Year's Mummer's Parade. There was a crippled man dragging a leg, a kid sporting brand-new Joe Lapchick sneakers, and a one-armed soldier with his sleeve pinned to his shoulder. There were two sailors with a 360-degree view of things and a marine just walking, eyes straight ahead as if on duty guarding the Unknown Soldier. (Man, did I love his uniform!) The whole tossed salad of humanity was there, walking up and down Market Street.

We worked our way up to Chestnut Street, and in the middle of the block Buster stopped suddenly. "This is it, Davey—the surprise," Buster said. "Horn & Hardart's, the most famous cafeteria in the world!"

He leaned on the gold-filigreed glass door until I passed through. Inside, a chubby patron stood off to the right, snapping flash shots with his Argus C3 camera—I owned one, so I knew. I was tempted to ask him to shoot a picture of me and Buster and send it to me, but his wife's hand motion hurried him into line. I queued up behind her massive girth, which eclipsed my view of everything before me as we inched along toward one of the glass-encased cashier booths. ("She could miss a hundred meals before her body alarm would signal the need for intake," I unkindly reflected to myself.)

We finally got to the front of the line, where a cashier stood waiting, rubber-tipped fingers poised for action. Buster laid a dollar bill on the marble counter in front of her, and she expertly shot 20 nickels forward through channeled slots. I dug into my pocket for one of Daddy Warbucks' remaining bills, put it down on the counter, and scooped up the minor avalanche of five-cent pieces that came my way. "They call those ladies nickel-throwers," Buster whispered to me as we walked away with our coins.

I followed Buster to a wall of shoebox-sized windows, behind which rested the choices of the day, ready for inserted nickels to spring them. I opted for a chicken pot pie, a seven-nickel choice. I hit the button, the window tilted up, and my hand went in and snagged my aromatic selection. Next an apple pie—three nickels.

The place was packed, but we finally found two seats at a table occupied by a gentleman wearing a frayed Stetson. He was a true isolationist, choosing to remain anonymous behind a vertically creased *Inquirer*, morning edition. He periodically reached finger and thumb around the printed page and found the handle on his coffee cup. After each small sip, he returned cup to saucer perfectly.

At the table to our left was a lady of more than middle age, pinning her broccoli to her plate with a fork, then cutting the stem three times before lifting it to her quivering lip. I halted my observations long enough to dispense with my victuals while Buster wolfed down his meatloaf, gravy-laden mashed potatoes, side order of noodles, and a buttered Kaiser roll.

Despite the heavy foot traffic along the line of cash-hungry windows, the pink marble floor sparkled. Buster grabbed my arm just as I took my last bite of cinnamon-scented apple pie. "Just enough time to catch the Mosconi match," he said with a grin.

At 15 I'd already felt the lure of the cue stick, and the name of Willie Mosconi flashed in my head with neon lights. Buster and I got to Market Street and 14th in less than 10 minutes, measurable by the giant clock on City Hall, and ran up the double flight of stairs to Allinger's

Billiard Academy, a Philadelphia institution located across the street from John Wanamaker's department store.

We paused at the door to check the layout of the room. Patrons sat in elevated chairs along the wall, watching action on any of 20 tables. Despite strategically placed spittoons, the worn linoleum floors were splotched with tobacco spittle. We headed toward the featured table, set off from all the others behind a thigh-high, gold-ringed, green velvet curtain.

To one side, bleachers were set up for the public to watch the match. We bought tickets, then found front-row seats in time to watch the warm-up session. Andrew "Ponzi" D'Alessandro led off, demonstrating his world-class status as he practiced bank shots, rail shots, and all the angles. Ponzi's framed photo hung on the wall of Royal Billiards back in Chester, and the written commentary under it stated that Ponzi's highest run in straight pool was 309 balls.

Ponzi then relinquished the table to Willie, who loosened up with an assortment of shots, showing cue ball control so deft that I felt I was in the presence of the maestro of exactness.

The referee silenced the crowd with a commanding voice, signifying the gravity of this officially sanctioned match between two of Philadelphia's greatest. This match was one in a series to determine who would reign as the pocket billiards champion of the world. After a respectful round of applause, both men took positions at the far end of the table, leaned forward in tandem, and stroked cue balls to hit the far rail and return. The "lag" was won by Mosconi, so Ponzi had to shoot first.

Ponzi stepped forward and called "safe." Willie then stepped to the table with the nonchalant expression of a short-order cook about to prepare his 300th ham omelet, circled the table to check the angles, then called out "two-ball, corner pocket." The referee echoed Willie's called shot. Willie leaned forward, stroked the cue ball four times, shot, and the two-ball disappeared into the corner pocket. The cue ball spun off the rail, hit the rack, and set up Willie's next shot.

I leaned forward in silent awe, elbows propped on my knees, chin supported by upturned palms, as Willie moved from shot to shot without frown or concern until he'd sunk 150 balls without missing. The game ended, 150-0. After exchanging a gentlemanly handshake with his compatriot, Willie unscrewed his two-piece cue, slid it into a black case, and then moved over to greet his line-up of well-wishers. I sat pondering whether I should walk up, stick out my hand, and feel the press of the most talented stroke in the world. But I resisted the urge, sitting in dumbstruck admiration until he finished acknowledging his fans and left with some local cronies.

As Buster led the way toward the exit, I let the present historic moment slide into past imperfect, but vowed that someday—don't know where, don't know when—Willie and I would meet in a match in a race to 150. Lost in this lofty thought, I tripped on the second step in descent. Once again coming to my rescue, Buster broke my forward fall down two flights by grabbing the rail as I slammed into his leg.

As we waited for the light to change, I glanced up at City Hall and noticed that the clock had clicked to 1:14. While Buster checked the train schedule he'd stuffed in his pocket, I transitioned from the glow of watching Mosconi execute total cue ball control to the reality of traffic and street cacophony.

"We've got an hour and a half till train time, Dave," Buster said. "Let's walk up the Parkway."

I agreed readily, though I didn't know what he

195

meant—that grand avenue not yet being a part of my limited experience. As we crossed onto the wide concourse surrounding City Hall, we heard an eerie shrill coming from the east sidewalk. Men decked out in plaid kilts and woolen knee-high socks were standing tall and proud, squeezing kidney-shaped bags under their arms. The wailing Gaelic sounds lodged in my psyche, a far cry from Louie's rhythm and blues. The last squeeze of the pipes reached my ears as we moved through the arched inner court.

We then angled to the tree-lined Parkway, walked to Logan Circle, and sat on a bench facing the fountain. Nannies pushed strollers on the wide cement walkway that surrounded the sculpted Greek god spouting water. Two senior citizens, in the glory of their twilight years, tossed crumbs to a congregation of barrel-chested pigeons hustling a free lunch. "Is this how it will be for me around the bend of years?" I wondered.

My eyes moved to the next bench, where an old man sat alone, legs extended, head resting on the back of the bench, hat slanting out the sun, a cigarette burning up toward his knuckle-clenched fist. "Is this another future option?" I mused.

I stood, stretched, then walked to the circular lip of the fountain and dipped my hands in the water. Skyward-sprayed bubbles danced in a rainbow spectrum before gravity's urge settled them back to the liquid pool circling my fingers. I looked over at City Hall crowned with Billy Penn's statue and wondered how they'd hoisted him up there. It made sense to have the Founding Father bless all who lived, moved, and enjoyed being in Philly. I even wondered why I wondered about things like that.

Observations, sounds of music (jazz, bagpipe, and street noise), anonymous faces, total strangers offering me hooky money—all these were forging new linkages in

196

my brain. Perhaps I really wasn't ready for the world I was growing into: street traffic moving at the speed of a track meet, people walking around knowing where they were going, even bums in the street seeming in total control of city life.

I turned slowly, counter-clockwise, to focus on the Cathedral of Saint Peter and Saint Paul. I stood speechlessly admiring the ageless architecture, then the courthouse, the Free Library, the Curtis Institute, the Museum of Natural History, the Ben Franklin Museum, and the crowning achievement of Greek-inspired architecture, the Philadelphia Art Museum.

As I sat in silent respect for the legacy left for us, Buster broke from his own reveries and said, "Gotta go, Davey. The train leaves in 20 minutes."

We loped across 18th, moving with purpose towards Market Street. Habit and instinct kept me from tripping on embedded manhole covers as my eyes scanned the passing crowd of urbanites: a pear-shaped man whose hips would easily overlap two seats on a bus; two nuns arm-locked at the elbows, perhaps to thwart an undignified stumble over uneven bricks; an uncollared dog lifting a leg and spraying a hydrant; a cop whistling a tune and swinging a mahogany club.

We crossed Arch Street, paved with Belgian blocks the size and shape of a loaf of bread, and Buster's relentless pace landed us at Suburban Station with five minutes to spare. I bought a Hershey almond bar at the concession stand, unpeeled it, and pocketed the wrapper. I broke it, handing halfers to Buster. We boarded a sparsely populated car, where I sat contently nibbling and indulging in daydreams until I was reanimated by Buster's nudge and the conductor's stentorian bellow, "Next stop Chester; Chester next station stop."

As my sneakered feet touched down on the splintered

wooden platform, Buster said, "Thanks for joining me, Davey. Let's hooky again sometime."

"Anytime, Buster," I agreed eagerly. "Maybe next Friday. We'll call it a field trip and check out everything on the Parkway."

Buster took off running down Sixth to his shoebox of a house on Crosby, while I headed for the YMCA, where today's fantasy trip had begun. Remnants of chicken pot pie and Hershey almonds intermingled in a burp as I turned onto Edgmont, lost in thoughts of the day's events. As I crossed Seventh, I saw brother George mounting the Y steps with his gym bag. Spotting me, he paused long enough to ruin my day by barking, "Where you been, Dave? Mom wants to know why you skipped school today. The truant officer made a house call looking for you—almost forced entry."

I gagged and crossed the street to join the bearer of bad news. Following my brother up the steps and into the lobby, I watched him flash his membership card at Mr. Wilson, who touched a buzzer springing the locker room door. As George disappeared, giving me a last unsympathetic glance, my thoughts shifted from remembered pleasure to anticipated pain. How now to explain the unexplainable to Mom? How now, Davey?

I trudged two flights to the recreation room, where I sat formulating my explanation to Mom's unavoidable question. Not finding one, I shot a couple of racks of eight-ball with Fred Parker. Before pocketing the eight-ball, I realized I was behind it—and plumbed the depths of my 15-year-old brain for some kind of answer, any kind of answer. Then it came to me!

I left for home, ready to face the music—although definitely not the kind I'd heard that morning at the Earle. As I hit the street, I saw Officer Kandravi rumbling down Edgmont on a motorcycle. It was approaching five o'clock when I opened the front door and eased down the hallway through two adjoining rooms to the kitchen, where Mom stood at the kitchen counter busying herself with pots and dishes.

I flashed my usual greeting, kissed her right temple, and waited for the big question. But first came a gentle query as to whether I was hungry.

"I'll make a meatloaf sandwich, Mom, if it's still in the fridge."

She nodded, then looked at me with her soft brown eyes and asked, "Where did you go today, Davey? The truant officer came by asking why you missed school."

My answer was clear and I thought convincing: "We took a field trip into Philly today, Mom. Maybe the attendance records got loused up, and the principal's office didn't know."

Mom gazed at me levelly and then turned to grind the lid off a can of Campbell 's tomato soup. Even with her back turned, I still felt those brown eyes on me. She nodded thoughtfully at my explanation and then scooped the soup into a pan, diluted it with water, and started warming it up. No cross-examination.

I ate the meatloaf sandwich, drank the soup, gave her a kiss on the forehead, and retreated to my room for socks, shorts, and clean shirt. Then I ran off to the Y, where I took a hot shower, changed into presentable duds, and sauntered off to the dance at Saint Michael's Church.

The evening events flowed as smoothly as Louie Armstrong's rendition of "Blueberry Hill." After coffee and a slab of Boston cream pie at the Boyd Diner with John Samara, Tony Minnetti, and Jimmy Orobono, I headed home happier than Frank Sinatra singing "When I Fall in Love."

In a flush of love, perhaps tinged with a little hint of bribery, I used some of Daddy Warbucks' remaining largesse to buy Mom a pint of Breyer's peach ice cream on the way. After kissing her goodnight, I mounted the shoulder-wide stairwell to my third-floor room. I slid between freshly washed sheets and clicked the light off, inviting dancing shadow patterns on the far wall, random patterns reflected by the mesh-screened streetlight. I listened as trolleys hissed an electrical cackle from the overhead line, listened as the off-key upright at the Eagle Bar eased the locals into a happy stupor, leading them in raucous, raised-mug songs in praise of the war's end.

All was well again in the Western world. Brother Mickey, brother John, brother Joe, brother Dan, and handsome Richard, courter and winner of the lovely hand of dear sister Victoria, all—Praise The LORD!—had returned home safely from the war.

I drowsed, but real sleep would not come. Pasted behind my closed eyelids were Mom's eyes staring into the inner sanctum of my soul—pasted there because I'd looked into those eyes earlier today and fibbed. I'd renamed a hooky a field trip. Mom's eyes remained long after the Eagle Bar closed and long after the last trolley passed my window into town.

Finally I drifted into a twilight zone and found myself in a sort of celestial night court. There a black-robed judge appeared, high and lifted up. I stood in the docket before the bench, raised my right hand, and touched the Bible with my left. When asked how I pleaded, I loudly stated, "Guilty, Your Honor, guilty with extenuating circumstances. And if I may, Your Honor, I'd like to explain those circumstances."

"Say on," said the judge. "Take your time, David. We have all night if need be. This is a serious offense you've committed, an offense against God, motherhood, and all that will follow in your lifetime."

And so I told my story of the day, told every detail as it came to me, told it with all the fervor and passion my narrow-gauged mental track could muster. I sat down, ready to take what was coming. But then I had an afterthought and sprang back to my feet.

"Your Honor, you were a kid once. I saw the sparkle in your eye when I talked about Buster saving my life, and when I told about my walk down Market Street, and when I tried to describe the Pied Piper sounds of Louie Armstrong. And, Your Honor, I did learn a lot today. I learned what a friend like Buster can do to open new doors to life. I learned about a total stranger wanting to bankroll a kid because it's what he just fought a war for. I learned things that can't be learned from math class or slicing a frog or memorizing earth elements from a chart."

I looked earnestly at the judge and saw that he was listening to me intently.

"I learned this, too, Your Honor. I learned that, despite all I enjoyed today, it's wrong to fib to my mom, especially when she looks at me with believing eyes. Yes, Your Honor, I plead guilty, and I also plead for forgiveness for fibbing into the face of innocence and a mother's trust. I rest my case."

I sat, my eyes focused on the judge's face. He was staring up at the chalk-white embellishments on the courtroom ceiling, but I had the feeling he was looking into his childhood memory room. In time, the gavel came down heavy.

The judge, looking me straight in the eye, said "This court finds you guilty as charged. Your punishment is as follows: You must move the ashes from cellar to curb every Wednesday from now till winter commences and, as earnings permit, buy your Mom a pint of hand-packed peach ice cream on Ash Night, directly after washing your hands. This court is adjourned."

Yes, yes, yes! I carried out the ashes every Wednesday until the first onslaught of winter, bought the hand-packed pint of peach from newspaper earnings every Wednesday at Charlie Peck's across the street, and henceforth told Mom the truth in response to all questions tendered.

I'll admit I had a slight lapse in conduct the following Monday when I ice-picked the rear tire of the truant officer's car parked in front of the post office at Fifth and Edgmont, but I felt this was just retribution for his attempt at forced entry when Mom had struggled to stave him off. Luckily the flat tire inquiry never came to our door, but the truant officer continued to pay regular visits until Paul and Jim graduated.

P.S. I did play Willie Mosconi in exhibition years later in California, and Willie unceremoniously did to me what he'd done to Ponzi that day. Well, not quite—I got four balls. I did eventually honor the memory of Daddy Warbucks by offering a fan of bills to a kid, but that's another story. And not until now, in writing, have I confessed to brother George that my Ash Wednesday routine (a duty previously shared with him on a biweekly basis) was not a noble deed on my part but rather one demanded by the judge. And, yes, Mom's eyes vanished from behind my lids after judgment was rendered, but as I write this I find myself wishing her eyes would return to visit once in a while.

Graduation Reverie

It was June 12, 1948. A double line of capped and gowned graduates was about to shuffle from the oppressive sunshine into the air-conditioned recesses of the Stanley Theatre. From my vantage point somewhere in the middle of the procession, the line looked like an 800-foot black caterpillar as it extended back to Fifth and Edgmont.

Sweat trickled down my back, finding its way into my socks, as the Class of '48 jabbered small talk and waited for the line to inch forward. I was horsing around on the pavement with my buddy Ralphie, our recently acquired zoot suits shrouded by the ceremonial black robes, when Mr. Sholley, my social studies teacher, grabbed us and nudged us to the front of the line. "Move it, Dave, move it," Ralphie said.

We solemnly shuffled on a slanting descent into the Stanley, moving down a 40-foot gradual slope through the mezzanine before proceeding through the embossed, polished brass doors into a rush of welcome coolness. Aisle by aisle, Mr. Plafker directed the seating, pointing Ralphie and me into the last row. (I later discovered that we were seated according to class standing.)

I edged my way to a plush, contoured seat in the rear, a seat angled to allow a profile view of most of my 400 classmates as they filed in. The theater filled slowly as the orchestra, conducted by Mr. Lewis R. Zelley, solemnized the seating of the graduating class. I cut the clowning and fell into a mesmerized search for the meaning locked in this never to be repeated moment.

The Stanley Theatre was Chester's most opulent arena, the darkened palace that lit up the lives of overworked citizens who willingly queued up for the chance to absorb all that Hollywood produced. The Stanley also hosted the big bands when they came to town—Tommy Dorsey, Kay Kyser, Stan Kenton. Bond drives had been held there during the war years, urging hard-earned money out of the blue-collar labor that had built a "victory ship" a week at Sun Ship Yard and 60 jeeps an hour at the Ford Motor plant. I sat in the theater weekly and suffered the pangs of vicarious passion as Jeanne Crain, Betty Grable, and Paulette Goddard reeled in their leading men with their beauty and allure.

The class moved to their seats slowly—12 years of my life and times, sitting shoulder to shoulder like a compressed accordion. We'd been through Larkin Grammar together, Smedley Junior High, then three meteoric years at Chester High. A tidal wave of memories filled my head as I scanned the theater. Some were like a color slide, some sepia-toned. Other memories were like an 8-millimeter movie and could run on and on if I let them.

How and when did our lives touch, if they touched at all? How did we grow through all the awkward struggles

204

in search of who we were at every stage and what we hoped to be?

During our childhoods, we'd measured our height by notches on the door jamb, and slowly, imperceptibly we grew—not just up but outward, like rings on a tree trunk. The concentric circles moved us from breastfeeding and the crib to crawling, to wobbly stance, to a toddler's strut that felt like balancing on stilts, then—magic!—to a hand-held walk to school with milk money in our pocket.

We quickly moved to a morning salute of the flag, to cursive with ink pen, to dodge ball at recess and marble games in the hand-smoothed dirt, to hide and go seek, to King of the Hill, to footraces, to fistfights, to pitching pennies, to crap-shooting in the alley.

Then we moved on to the YMCA where we swam naked in a chlorinated pool, to gym class where we tumbled on mats and climbed ropes hand-over-hand to the ceiling, to the Village Green Pool where we learned how to flip a one-and-a-half gainer off the 9-foot board and swim two lengths under water. We tossed medicine balls and played basketball, handball, baseball, football in the mud, stickball, volleyball, and sometimes the sissy games of badminton and tennis.

I did all this and more, as the circles of my tree trunk added impervious bark, taking me from diapers to short pants, to knickers to Levi's and church suits, to zoot suits and tailor-made shirts with Billy Eckstein collars. And between the growing circles, I felt my sap rise and my strength increase. My limbs of experience reached nimbly out, further and further, until all the wards in Chester were known to my migratory feet. I carried my passport under my left arm and flashed it with my right—huckstering the nightly news wherever I could sniff out a sale.

Casting my mental meanderings aside, I glanced

around again at the 400 capped and gowned kids gathered in the Stanley. Together and individually we'd suffered the agonies and enjoyed the ecstasies, and along the way we'd begun to question for ourselves who we were, where we came from, and where we would be headed when earthly life came to an end. But right now it was childhood that was ending, and we were about to step out into the arena of life beyond Chester High.

In the orchestra pit, Bob Barkley lowered his chinned violin, Roland Cohen unpuckered his clarinet, and the saxophone section unclipped their neck hooks. Mr. Zelley lowered his baton to his side, ending the orchestral repetitions of pomp as the verbal circumstances were about to begin.

Silence reigned as the Reverend Richard Strohman of Third Presbyterian Church invoked heaven's blessings upon us all, and then Principal Karl Agan strode into position center-stage and sought to homogenize the gathering with upbeat positivism. After a spirited crescendo of handclaps, Principal Agan returned to his seat among the dignitaries seated at stage-right.

It was during the superintendent's speech that my focus clouded. His commentary had the effect of swallowing a bowl of shredded wheat with no milk, so I opened my yearbook for some distraction from the stage proceedings. I fingered the pages randomly until I came to the double-page spread of a cartoon Ferris wheel in which sat the "Big Wheels" of the Class of '48, their faces as recognizable as the Coca Cola logo.

There was Fred Parker up near the top. "That's where you belong, Fred, even though my influence sometimes led you astray. We shared the same neighborhood, the same mentors, for 12 years. Remember when we got booted from the basketball team by Coach Forwood when we missed the school bus home from the Radnor game?"

And there was Harry Ashbridge in the next seat. "You couldn't do better than date Bennie Holcomb's sister. You've got my seal of approval on that one."

And Poe Parramore: "You're the dream of every mother who prays on bended knee that her daughter will marry you and improve the human race by 12 or more."

And just below him was Harold Stewart looking suave: "Harold, your face should be plastered on every mannequin in Adam's Clothing Store's display windows. They'd sell more suits."

And there was Walt Pietryka: "Walt, if you don't rip any tendons scooping wild pitches out of the dirt, I'll be paying someday to see you play for the Phillies."

My thoughts drifted back to the hot August day when I'd faced Barney Massi in a Saturday afternoon pick-up game on the dirt field behind the Deshong Museum. I'd just gulped down a mini bottle of Miller Flounders chocolate milk before stepping to the plate as confident as Ferris Fain, fearless first baseman for the A's. And then Barney's fastball connected just below my left ear, driving me face down in the dust. As I limped to first base, I told myself that Barney might have a mean streak but he surely hadn't meant to clobber me. Next time up, his fastball bounced off my rib cage just above the kidney—permanently closing the door on my Major League fantasies.

A ripple of applause for the speech I'd been tuning out snapped me back to my seat in the back row of the Stanley. From the podium, Vice Principal Giles declared, "And now for the long-awaited moment of the presentation of diplomas." The leatherette-encased diplomas were placed in stacks (hopefully in the right order) to the side of the stage near the stairs so that the recipients could make a quick descent after a hearty handshake from Principal Agan.

As the roster of graduates was called out, I amused myself by listening for butchered pronunciation of the Slavic names and watched for a while the slow saunters across the stage followed by the brisk walks back to assigned seats. I figured it would be a long wait before my name was called, so I returned to the Ferris wheel picture at the back of the yearbook.

There was Art Levy: "Hey, Art, if you follow in your brother's footsteps you're destined for respect in the highly buffed hallways of the county courthouse. But I'll still always remember you as the guard who passed the ball for cut shots and made Herky Miller's game look good."

And George Weiss: "I always saw you hunched over an encyclopedia at the Crozer Library on Ninth Street. I hope the hound dog pursuit of knowledge doesn't keep you from smelling the roses."

And Anna Mae Fuhrman: "I watched you bounce and gyrate down the halls of Smedley and Chester High for six years. Maybe it was your heel spins and quick steps that inspired my jitterbugging skills."

The announced names began to reverberate from the chandeliers as the lengthy list of grads was summoned one by one to the stage. I returned to my yearbook, zooming in on Lee Layton, whose placid face belied the Swiss-watch timing of his wit. "We shared Smedley for three years, Lee, as well as the love of pool and the lure of a deck of cards."

And there's Anne Hughes, smiling. Could it be she's thinking of the night I'd walked her home from the Smedley eighth-grade dance?

There are Barry Ives and Audrey Cullis, two of the smartest kids in the class: "While you humbly bowed to the Oracle of Knowledge for answers to life's riddles, I, on the other hand, majored in minors of no consequence."

And Pat Nolan: "You vibrate health! Your face should adorn a Wheaties box."

And here was Joe Tiburzi: "Joe, your feats on a mud-patched football field will forever hang in memory."

Reflecting on Joe's stellar accomplishments reminded me of my own short-circuited football career, which abruptly ended when I was a sophomore. At practice one day, I returned a kick and my hip pads slipped around and caught my groin, grounding me without a tackle. Coach Babe Buono didn't come right out and say it, but I could see it in his eyes: "You do not possess the 'Try to get around my end' attitude your brother George had—not to mention brother Dan's back-field "Bronco Nagurski" feats in '44."

And so, reluctantly, I traded in my jock for a shoehorn and a part-time job at A. S. Beck on Market Street. This, I rationalized, put coins in my pocket, thereby funding my poolroom acumen, which in turn reaped dividends to buy tailor-made zoot suits such as the one adorning me now.

I closed the yearbook just in time to heed the call of my mispronounced name. (Being eighth in the family to attend Chester High, you'd think they'd get it right by now). This disgruntled thought kept me company down the aisle and across the stage to receive my diploma and a handshake, eye contact, and congratulations from Principal Agan. I then skipped down the steps like Fred Astaire and breezed back to my seat.

It took a while for the roll call to get from "Komarnicki" to "Zultowski," but the procession finally ended, and it was time for Ralph McCafferty to step to the podium and deliver the valedictory speech. His tone was fittingly elevated and he tossed off a lot of four-syllable words, but they didn't do much to capture my rapidly dwindling attention.

209

In finale, we stood to sing the "Star Spangled Banner," stitching a hem on the woven memories of 1945-48, and then, like a giant whale, the Stanley Theatre belched out the sons and daughters of Chester.

I was among the last to exit into the afternoon sunlight. After exchanging wisecracks and small talk and looking into faces I knew I'd never see again, I defrocked, tucking the ceremonial garb under my arm, and began walking with a straight-backed strut up Edgmont toward town—ready for the potluck of life.

Afterword

Up and down the streets of Chester—and up and down the streets of every city and town in America back in the early 40s—there were "sons in service" flags in the windows. These flags were not just statements of patriotism but also reminders of the flesh-and-blood loved ones living in harm's way so the rest of us could remain free. They were symbols of the fathers and husbands and brothers we prayed for daily and wanted desperately to have back with us when the enemy was defeated and the war was over.

Our particular flag had five stars, representing my oldest brother, Michael (or "Mickey"), who entered the army in 1942 and spent the war years in Burma; brother John, who enlisted in the Navy in 1943 and served in the Pacific; Joe, who joined the Air Force in 1943 and spent the war as a pilot and flight instructor; brother Dan, who joined the Navy in 1944 and also served in the Pacific; and our brother-in-law Richard, who entered the Army in 1942 and was stationed in England.

By the grace of God, they all came back alive—not just alive but unscathed. And they all went on to lead productive lives, just as we all did—some right near Chester where we grew up, others of us in more distant fields.

Top row, left to right: Michael ("Mickey"), John, Joe
Bottom row, left to right: Dan, Richard

Over the years, the family Komarnicki remained a tight circle. Those who lived in the area gathered for monthly Bible studies, and every New Year's Eve the geographically distant siblings gathered up their own families and came home by plane or car for the annual festivities of good food, good talk, and good-natured, fun-poking skits.

Time, of course, has changed the balance of those

212

living here on earth and those enjoying fellowship in heaven. Pop was the first to leave us, being snatched up one afternoon in 1958 at the age of 65. He was in the middle of prayer with two Christian friends when suddenly his voice went silent. Mom lived on for another 15 years, making her home with sister Mary and her husband, Jimmy Turk.

Brother Mickey, who had been plagued with cancer since the war, died way too young—passing away in 1980 at the age of 61. His wife, Myra, with whom he had roller-skated at the Great Leopard all those years ago, died just four years later. Their small row home in Ridley was always a center of hospitality, and Mickey was famous for his red convertible, his cole slaw, his love for the Phillies, and his sweet smile.

Brother John spent his working life as a boiler-maker at Sun Ship and was a symbol of strength and integrity to all who knew him. In retirement, his daily routine included a five-mile walk along Chester Creek and into Linvilla and another walk in Market Square Memorial Park in Marcus Hook. He died suddenly in 2004 of a heart-related cause, leaving a big John-sized hole in all our lives. He was followed in death by his wife, Eileen, in 2005.

Sister Vicky died in 2008, of a broken heart as much as anything else. Her whole adult life had been spent in sweet tandem with her husband, Richard Helm. Their later years were a happy mix of golfing, traveling, and puttering around their Wallingford home in quiet contentment. Richard's death in 2000 took the joy out of Vicky's life, but we all still took joy and delight in her.

Shockingly, the youngest of us all was the next to leave our circle. Brother Jim, the only one of us to earn a doctorate, enjoyed a long career as an education professor at Regent University in Virginia Beach and was taken from us in 2008 at the age of 73. Jim, despite what you'd expect from a man with an advanced degree, was the clown of the family and creator of most of the New Year's skits. His effervescent wife, Barbara, still lives in Virginia Beach.

The next to leave us was the one we called the "matriarch"—dear sister Mary, the firstborn, who lived to a glorious 92 years old before joining her loved ones in glory in 2010. She outlived her husband, Jimmy Turk, by nearly 30 years, staying in their Brookhaven home and welcoming generations of the Komarnicki clan to lovingly prepared feasts around her dining table at Thanksgiving and laughter-filled reminiscing around her kitchen table any day of the year.

Nearly three years passed before our numbers were again diminished. Brother George, the next one up from me in the sibling ranks, left us in January 2013 at the age of 84. He was the world traveler among us and was enjoying a peripatetic lifestyle almost to the end. Three years after the death of his adored wife, Marigrace, he sold their big home in Radnor (venue of most of the New Year's Eve parties over the years), and spent his time visiting friends and family on both coasts and traveling to his beloved England at least once a year.

Just two Novembers ago, in the early hours of Thanksgiving morning, Joe left us to join his wife—sweet, sparkling Doris, whom he wooed and won in high school—in God's eternal kingdom. Joe served Chester High as class president, Bell Telephone as an executive, and our family as the personification of honor and dependability. He was 89 and as handsome as ever when he died.

Paul, who occupied the rung just below me, was taken from us on June 24, 2015, after a long struggle with Parkinson's disease. Throughout their long marriage, Paul and his wife, Kim lived in the same log home that they moved into in the early 1950s, when he took a

214

position as a schoolteacher in Pines Lake, New Jersey. Until Paul fell ill, he and Kim were always on the go, traveling up and down the East Coast and across the country to visit family and old friends. They enjoyed a full and active life, taking pleasure in their church, their neighbors, their kids, and their grandkids.

Only two of the original 10 are still living, still sharing our memories with children and grandchildren and telling them what it was like to grow up Komarnicki in the patchwork quilt of Chester before and during the war years.

Dan is 90, still handsome, and enjoying retirement in Clearwater, Florida. He pioneered the Young Life movement in the southern US, spending many years in North Carolina, and in recent years has enjoyed re-meeting many of the men and women he led to Christ as teenagers.

As for me, after a nearly 30-year detour in California, I moved back to Pennsylvania in 1986 with my wife, Leslie, and our two young daughters. My work life in California was spent in teaching, both as a public-school teacher and as a financial trainer. I now concentrate most of my time on our mission, Disciples International. Our daughters, Elizabeth and Amy, are grown and have given us four beautiful grandsons.

And, as it happens, life has come full circle for me. Leslie and I moved to Chester—place of my birth and setting of all the stories in this book—in 1999 and have lived here for the past 17 years. I can still almost walk my paper route and still almost smell the aroma of Texas Wieners and the inner sanctums of the taprooms.

Life has strange twists, but God is good.

David Komarnicki, December 2016

215